A. Okechukwu Ogbonnaya, Ph.D., School of Theology at Claremont, serves as Pastor of St. John's United Methodist Church in Watts, Los Angeles. He has lectured across the nation on theological issues relating to African thought systems and serves as adjunct faculty for the University of La Verne Extension program at the Ecumenical Center for Black Church Studies.

ON COMMUNITARIAN DIVINITY

An African Interpretation of the Trinity

A. OKECHUKWU OGBONNAYA

Paragon House
New York

First Edition, 1994

Published in the United States by

Paragon House
370 Lexington Avenue
New York, NY 10017

Library of Congress Cataloging-in-Publication Data

Ogbonnaya, A. Okechukwu (Aloysious Okechukwu)
  On communitarian divinity : an African perspective of the Trinity
  by A. Okechukwu Ogbonnaya.—1st ed.

    p.   cm.
  Includes bibliographical references and index.
  ISBN 1-55778-704-2
  1. Trinity.   2. Theology, Doctrinal—Africa.   3. Religion and
  sociology—Africa.   4. Community—Philosophy.   5. Tertullian, ca.
  160-ca. 230—Contributions in doctrine of the Trinity.   6. Trinity—
  History of doctrines—Early church, ca. 30-600.   I. Title.
  BT111.2.O4   1994
  231'.044—dc20   94-12161
                                                                 CIP

Manufactured in the United States of America

*This book is dedicated to the memories
of my paternal and maternal grandparents
and father-in-law Njomu Nwani Ngene.*

Contents

Acknowledgments

To write a book of this nature one needs a community to help guide, correct, and comfort one through the process. My belief in African community was formed—long before I heard the word theology—by a communal experience of belonging among my people and various African peoples. This sense of community, as my *Chi* (spiritual guide) would have it, included the ancestors, spirits, and other beings within both my immediate cosmos and beyond. I was taught that I was connected with all and the All was connected to me.

Theology is divination. It is divining our way through the various experiences of the world with which we are privileged to have. A diviner is always an apprentice in the world. In this book I have tried to divine a way of thinking and talking about the Divine. In this process I have received help from many persons. I am grateful to the Dr. Elmer J. Thiessen professor of ethics and philosophy at Medicine Hat College, Alberta, Canada; Dr. John Cobb who was kind enough to look through the first and second drafts and to make some suggestions; Dr. David Griffin who also looked at an earlier draft; Dr. Mary Elizabeth Moore who chaired my doctoral dissertation committee; Dr. Karen J. Torjesen; my long time friend, Dr. Elias J. Mbaabu, who is always there to help me clarify a thought; and all my African colleagues at the Claremont School of Theology consortium. I am grateful to Dr. Vincent Wimbush for reading the manuscript and to Dr. Cain Hope Felder for listening to my musings on the telephone; to Alfred and Marianne Bohr of Canada for helping me begin the realization of my educational process; and to Michael Giampaoli and the staff at Paragon House for their support. Several people have supported me through my studies and through much of my undertakings. However, I am solely responsible for the esoterism found within the pages of this book. I am especially grateful for the support of my family, my wife Chinyere, my children Okwuchukwu, Amara, Kenechi, Nnamdi-ugo and to my family in Africa

I hope those who read this work will divine communality and by so doing dream a new way of being in the world.

Okechukwu,
Los Angeles, 1994

Introduction

This book explores, from an African communal worldview, the idea of the Trinity as found in the work of Tertullian. The examination of the concept of the Divine in its African context is meant to propose a new way of seeing and speaking about the Divine. An African worldview is brought to bear upon the Tertullian's historical formulation of the Trinity. My assumption is that Tertullian's theological enterprise needs to be examined in the context of African worldview. Such an analysis of the Trinity, which is the ultimate symbol of Divinity for much of Christendom, has particular relevance to theological discourse today.

This book is meant to do a number of things. First, to call into question the manner in which the discourse about the Divine has proceeded and to join the ranks of those who are calling for a new way to envision and speak of the Divine. Second, to show African contribution to Christianity through the influences of Tertullian. Third, to correct some misconceptions about African religious thought created by attempts to fit traditional African thought into Western models, while ignoring essential African categories. Fourth, to correct the misunderstanding that North African Christianity is essentially separated or absolutely disconnected from African thought. Fifth, to show that this connection is important for understanding and doing Christian theology in Africa.

A reconsideration of Divinity from this perspective has implications for human community. It is almost a truism to say that how one conceives and speaks of God affects the way one lives with other human beings. But this statement is meant to affect the discourse on God that is being carried on in theological circles. Feminist theologians have also brought to the fore of theological discourse the idea that language about God affects how society treats women.

Human subjectivity, not divine objectification, is the source of knowledge both of the world and of the Divine.[1] In proposing a theory of divinity what is called for is not a transference of conceptual frames of other societies whether biblical or European but a conceptualization of the Divine based on the experience of the people. A conception based on the way a people live with one another and deriving from their various modes of being in the world. As Joseph Bracken states, "the mind as such is pure activity and its nature as pure activity can only be grasped reflexively in intuiting the primordial unity of the subject and object within human consciousness."[2] However, even many of the so-called radical theologians still fall into the concept of God that maintains and refines the oppressive patterns of Divination rather than transforming the underlying Eurocentric nature of the discourse on the Divine.

Some African scholars still carry on the discourse as though a monotheistic conception of the Divine is fundamental. Many oppressed peoples, African for example, seem to criticize the conception of the Divine imposed on them by the West, but fail to make an alternative proposal that is truly liberating. African scholars, nonetheless, proceed to speak of the Divine in the same way as their Eurocentric counterpart. In order for theological discourse or God-talk to change, Africans must begin using their own experience and traditional philosophical "categories." It will not do to discuss "African concepts" and then to turn around and present more of the same Eurocentric perspective unchanged by the discussion. When the conversation is carried on without the clear understanding that African concepts have radical implications for today's theological enterprise, African modes of thought are then seen as artifacts—much like the cultural artifacts from Africa that one finds in the houses of former missionaries having no positive corrective ideological or theological impact on the way they view Africa or Africans. Not only does this way of doing theology continue the cycle of hermeneutical bondage to which so many are subjected, it stifles the imagination and, hence, robs Africans of their authentic contribution to theological discourse. An example of this is the way African theologians all seem to speak positively of the African ideal of communality. This ideal, however, is not brought to bear on the discourse of the nature of God.

It is the aim of this work to bring this aspect of the African mode of being in the world to the conversation about the nature of the Divine. The first chapter will look at some ways in which community has been defined, drawing attention to distinctive African understanding of community. Chapter two will examine various theories about the Concept of God in Africa. The third chapter presents a classical example of African

Divinity. This chapter is deliberately somewhat repetitious because it is being used as exemplification of the concepts presented in chapter four. In the Chapter I present what I consider to be traditional African understandings of the Divine as Background to an African worldview analysis of Tertullian's Trinity. The fourth and fifth chapters focus on an analysis of Tertullian's theory of Divinity as seen through its African worldview. In chapter four, I will explore the various ways of conceiving the Divine that were available in Christianity around second century C.E. as found in Tertullian's work. Chapter five will look at the various social cultural Concepts used by Tertullian in his discourse on the Divine nature. It continues the presentation of Tertullian's theory of Divinity in its African framework. This examination is seen in light of the pervasive communality of the African cultures. Chapter six presents an epilogue.

AFRICAN COSMOLOGY AS BACKGROUND TO TERTULLIAN

An African understanding of the cosmos and the gods will be used to examine the Trinitarian work of Tertullian. Tertullian was an African church father who lived during the second century C.E. in North Africa, so his task is grounded in an African communal understanding of the Divine and of humanity. I will show that an African communal understanding of the Divine provides an adequate ground for: (1) explaining the meaning of equality; and (2) clarifying personal distinction and temporal subordination within community without subjecting differences to ontological inferiority. In order to provide a frame that is grounded in communal worldview orientation, a paradigmatic analysis of the Divine, from an African perspective, needs to be undertaken.

Heidegger has criticized Christian theology for confusing being and God.[3] This criticism is particular poignant for a religion that defines God in personal terms. African worldview with its emphasis on being transcends the cause-effect, inner-outer internal-external relationship and assuages the parochial tendency to define the world mainly in terms of anthropragmatic usefulness. By an emphasis on being as nonpersonalistic and yet personalizing, the African worldview offers a mode of conceiving the world that does not confuse rational will with the ground of being, which is spirit. Accordingly,

> Spirit as an immanent capacity for self-determination is likewise
> operative within actual occasions constitutive of inanimate realities

such as rocks and crystals. Similarly, it is the ontological principle within actual occasions making up plants and lower level animal organisms lacking in consciousness. Hence, contrary to what might be considered a major presupposition of modern Western philosophy, spirit and consciousness are not synonymous. A measure of spirit is to be found in every actual occasion and in every society to which it belongs, whether that society be the reality of an atom or the reality of highly complex animal organism such as human being.[4]

The distinction between God and gods or the desire to make God one and thus dismiss the existence of the gods is grounded in the confusion between being and God, as Heidegger has pointed out. This problem is played out acutely in the way African theologians deal with the concept of God. Much more than that, I think that the doctrine of the Trinity, if seen from an African communal perspective, will go a long way in providing ways to deal with this problem.

Several African writers have tried to contribute to the ongoing theological discussion particularly in relation to the idea of God. E. Bolaji Idowu and John Mbiti, for example, have targeted the concept of God as the starting point for such theologizing. In his *African Traditional Religion,* Idowu rightly observes that in African traditional religion, a common thread runs throughout it, which the term "negritude will express aptly."[5] The idea according to Idowu is the idea of God. However, what is important for this discussion is what Idowu says about the African concept of God. Idowu states:

> With regard to the concept of God, there is a common thread, however tenuous in places, running throughout the continent. Whatever outsiders may say, it is in fact this one factor of the concept, with reference to the "character" of Deity, which makes it possible to speak of a religion of Africa.[6]

It is true that the idea of the nature of God may be a common thread running through African consciousness, but the problem that faces African scholars is to determine the most adequate way of articulating the traditional African concept of the Divine. Various explanations have been offered; the two most prominent have been monotheism (the belief that there is only one God or that there is only one true God) and polytheism (the belief in many gods who are separate from one another). This book proposes a third, namely, the Divine as a community of gods. This concept of community pervades the African consciousness and can be discerned in classical Africa, Egypt for example, and in present traditional thought systems. My contention that the African concept of the Divine is communal is the atmosphere in which the whole discussion is to be understood. The problem of "God" and gods can be placed in historical context of the development of Christian theology in early African Christianity.

THE PROBLEM IN HISTORICAL PERSPECTIVE

Tertullian's historical-cultural situation allowed him to develop a particular conception of the Divine as community—one which enhances ontological equality, personal distinctiveness within the Divine, and a functional subordination among the persons of the Trinity that is temporal rather than ontological.

Tertullian, as a convert from African religions of his time, developed a concept of Divinity in his work on the Trinity that will be shown, upon analysis, to shed new light on the idea of the Divine as community without sacrificing the uniqueness of each communal member. Tertullian's concept of Divinity holds in dynamic interplay the idea of ontological equality, personal distinction, and functional-temporal subordination. Tertullian's emphasis on Divine communality was eclipsed, however, by the debates that ensued after his death, which fostered concepts of ontological hierarchy instead of equality.

Historically, the debate between the Orthodox and the so-called heretical party represented by *homousian* and *homoiousian* parties, respectively, failed to get to the heart of the matter, as both assumed a hierarchical paradigm. The Orthodox party, with its idea of eternal generation, created an eternal ontological hierarchy, while Arians maintained that the substance of one particular member was inferior to the other members of the Divine community. The Arian were a group of theologians in the second century B.C.E. who followed a man named Arius and grounded their thought in a phrase used by Tertullian. Tertullian maintained in *Adversus Praxeas* that "there was time when the Son was not." The Arians failed to understand the concept of communal ontological equality, which was fundamental to understanding this statement by Tertullian. Interestingly, Tertullian never refers to the Trinity as mystery. In his view, there is nothing mysterious about a god having a child or children. This assumption of mystery, particularly in relation to Divine progeny, underlies much of the trinitarian debate in the West—which was limited by the sociocultural framework that seemed to demand a hierarchical interpretation of the

Trinity. Neither the Greek metaphysical hierarchy nor Roman juri-prag-matic worldviews, which became the basis of western conceptualizations of the Divine, can serve as the adequate grounds for explaining Tertullian's understanding of the Trinity. Further, the debate neglected the sociocultural framework of Tertullian in which his understandings of the Trinity made sense. Recapturing this sociocultural framework, by looking at Tertullian from an African worldview perspective, will provide some benefits for a communal mode of interaction that have been neglected by continual domination of a Eurocentric worldview.

It is not surprising that early modern western scholars, also informed by Greek metaphysics, had difficulty accepting the doctrine of Divine plurality. During the eighteenth century, Immanuel Kant (1724–1804), expressing his position on the doctrine stated:

> The doctrine of the Trinity provides nothing, absolutely nothing, of value, even if one claims to understand it; still less when one is convinced that it far surpasses human understanding.[7]

Friedrich Schleiermacher (1768–1804), affirmed and proclaimed the Trin-ity while insisting that the idea of plural personalities in the Divine prior to creation cannot serve as "the necessary pre-condition of faith in redemption and in the founding of the Kingdom of God by means of the Divine in Christ and the Holy Spirit."[8] Schleiermacher expressly states that no matter how elaborately worked out, such a doctrine of the Trinity cannot be foundational for Christian dogmatics. The Trinity serves as the culmination of salvific history. Schleiermacher, by methodological ingenuity, relegated the idea of plurality within the Divine to the end of dogmatics. In this way, he safeguarded the idea of Divine Monad, which existed before creation. His conclusion was based on the conviction that the idea of an internal distinction in the Supreme Being is not an "utterance concerning religious consciousness."[9] For Schleiermacher, the Trinity is seen in terms of the Sabellian notion of redemptive history. The basic internal plurality of the Godhead prior to creation, which will be shown to be present in Tertullian's thought, is rejected for the distinction that occurs within creation and at the end of history.[10] As a result of the tone set by many nineteenth-and twentieth-century thinkers, the Trinity, or any reference to plurality within the Divine, became suspect and is stigmatized from the beginning as superstitious.*

Interest in the problem of the plurality of persons within the Godhead was renewed and intensified by the publication of Karl Barth's *Church Dogmatics* (1936). Barth insisted that the doctrine of the Trinity must be the basis of theological discourse.[11] This renewed interest spurred several scholars to investigate the implications of the idea of the Trinity for human life, including Jürgen Moltmann. In 1980, Moltmann published his *Trinity and the Kingdom,* where he bemoans the fact that the doctrine of the Trinity has been neglected by various models of contemporary theological discourse (e.g., hermeneutical, political, process, doctrinal). For Moltmann, the doctrine of the Trinity as a symbol of plurality has implications for the manifestation of the Kingdom of God on earth. The manner of the formulation of the doctrine also has great implications for the perception and exercise of human freedom within society.[12]

This renewed interest has also resulted in works on the Trinity by such authors as James P. Mackey, William J. Hill and others.[13] Of additional interest is the work of Raimundo Pannikar and Ewert Cousins. Pannikar approaches the doctrine from an interreligious and intercultural perspective. Pannikar's experience in both Hinduism and Christianity gives him a unique perspective on the trinitarian idea. Cousins also approaches the idea of the Trinity from a pluralistic perspective.[14]

LIBERATION THEOLOGIANS AND COMMUNAL THEOLOGY

A more recent wave of theologizing has come from communal perspectives. Among those who have argued for a communitarian orientation in the articulation of the Christian dogma is John Schanz, *A Theology of Christian Community.* Juan Luis Segundo, *A Theology for the Artisan of a New Humanity*, approaches theological anthropology from a communitarian perspective. Leonardo Boff and Joseph Bracken deal with the concept of God in its trinitarian formulation.

Liberation theology has contributed to some extent to this discussion on the Divine plurality and human society. Leonardo Boff's work, *Trinity and Society,* sets forth the idea of the Trinity as a prototype of human community. The Trinity, for Boff, has social and political implications,

---

* The tone for this was set by the post-Hegelian philosophical theologians e.g., Ludwig Ferrerbach (1804–1972) Albretch Ritschl (1822–1889) and those who followed them. See James C. Livingstone, *Modern Christian Thought: From Enlightenment to Vatican II* (New York: McMillan, 1971)

especially in providing a model of inclusiveness and communion in communities where similarities and differences are present. The Trinity can
also serve "both as a critique and inspiration of society," becoming the
"basis for an inclusive universal fellowship."[15] Thus, the Trinity, as a
symbol of unity in diversity, illuminates what it means to be a just and
truly humane society. For Moltmann, Boff, Pannikar, and Cousins, the
Trinity is an answer to the problem of pluralism confronting our generation.
But does the Trinity, in the way it has been understood and interpreted
in the West, really represent openness? The worldviews of peoples inter-
preting the doctrine has sometimes made it more of a paradigm for exclu-
sion and social intolerance.

JOSEPH BRACKEN'S COMMUNAL ANALYSIS OF THE TRINITY AND AFRICAN WORLDVIEW

Among the works on the Trinity, Joseph Bracken has done a much
more profound communal analysis of the theological concept. Within his
two revolutionary works, an African scholar may find many points of
agreement and help, but one who is attuned to the African worldview
will also find, seeping through the work, some problems.[16] Bracken sees
collective substance as opposed to individual substance as the bases for
community, not supra-individuality.[17] The definitive concept for analyzing
the Trinity from Bracken's perspective is society. Society is a preconsti-
tuted "environment." Even in writing about the Trinity Bracken assumes
monotheism and from that point tries to show that this one is three. It is
sometimes assumed that this oneness must be embodied completely in
one so as to support monotheism. Tertullian played with this idea while
at the same time proposing an egalitarian conception of the Trinity. It is
precisely this refusal to separate the inner and outer and the insistence
that no one single actual person embodies the divine totality that predis-
poses the African worldview as a basis for discussing the Trinity.

It is necessary to reconceive "the God-world relation in terms of interre-
lated fields of human activity within which the three divine persons and
all their creatures continuously come into being and are related to one
another."[18] Arguing against the uni-personalistic theism of Whiteheadian
philosophy and theology, Bracken proposes that "the three divine persons
should be understood as personally ordered society of occasions and that
their unity as one God is the unity of a Whiteheadian structured society
or society of subsocieties."[19]

Bracken considers "Society, as the ongoing field of activity or social environment, [that] preserves the pattern of interrelatedness for successive generations of actual occasions."[20] Some questions still remain to be addressed. For instance, what is the ontological basis of society that allows this preservation of generational interrelatedness? Or does this way of stating issues not force one into the placement of fundamental connection on functional rather than ontological ground? For the African, Ontology is not exactly distinguishable from ontology. Bracken, of course, considers

> The occasion themselves to be sure, by their de facto interrelatedness from moment to moment may gradually modify that pattern. But it still remains true that while actual occasions come and go, societies endure, the field of activity remains constant even though its constituents are continually renewed.[21]

From my own African philosophical perspective, I believe that internal relations demand that these be something more than the environment as the field of activity unless environment is defined as the totality that does not presuppose the old external/internal dichotomy that has characterized a major strand of western Christian philosophy. Change that begins with one localized phenomena becomes distributed to all the constituent or actual occasions within a given sphere because there is a basic contemporary principle of communality. But, for the foregoing statement to be accepted, several points must be present in the argument if it is considered from an African-Centered Perspective:

1. That the communal principle is considered a shared environment. But shared environment does not necessarily create connection that is lasting and communal. Unless the environment is somehow impressed upon the basic genetic interrelation of the members as actual entities within the environment. But community is not mainly a matter of mere genetic interconnection it is more a matter of the spirituo-genetic bindings created in and sustained by a communal mode of being in and seeing the world. Bracken says that "the element of order or patterns of intelligibility is due to the genetic interrelatedness of the members' actual entities."[22] This will fit well with the African concept of fundamental connection which will be used to advance the Trinity.
2. As the Community is prior to and also outlasts individual entities within it, this genetic structure must be consistent and perpetual. That is it must not change or if it changes its change must be so minuscule that its effect is not

noticeable for large epochs. Thus communal connection and consistency becomes another criteria for examining the Model of God.

3. Or, it must be shown that there is an ontological connection beyond genetic structures binding the disparate parts together even in their seeming individuality. Within, this African worldview this is attributable to some kind of spirit or soul that one may not be able to measure or dissect. This soul or spirit through some kind of centrifugal dynamism is able to multiply itself yet at the same time retaining its basic characteristic of inherent connection to its parts.

Though, I do not agree with Bracken on every count, he has been the most explicit in dealing with the Trinity from a communal philosophical perspective. It is quite accurate, in my opinion, to insist that the "notion of persons and community do apply to the doctrine of the Trinity with more coherence and plausibility."[22] Since sociologist, anthropologist, and theologian who have studied African cultures have determined that the notion of communality is fundamental to the ways Africans view the world, looking at the Trinity from an African perspective might have something to offer.

Methodologically, the emphasis on communality allows theologizing to be seen in terms of humanity rather than the false claim that it is from the perspective of the total Divine community. Bracken, writing from the perspective process philosophy in the tradition of Alfred North Whitehead, has lifted up many important insights for analyzing the doctrine of Trinity. Though I do not use his terms and concepts explicitly within the work, I want the reader to be aware of the debt I owe Bracken's work as dialogue partner.

However, while providing some innovative ways of seeing the Trinity, the traditional emphasis on the Father as an eternally unaffected ontological principle remains. Bracken sees "the father as the source of all life and being." His emphasis on community not withstanding, he is still left with a patricentric Trinity. For him the "Father expresses himself perfectly in the Son through the Holy Spirit." His use of such terms as "the father expresses," "the son responds," "through the holy spirit," though theologically insightful nonetheless seems to continue the idea of the Trinity that I think needs to be changed. For him these functions are in no means exchangeable. He falls, it seem to me, into what I term the fallacy of functional ontology. Research has shown clearly that ultimate ontological reality is a social, not an individual entity. For a long time the dominant interpretation of the idea of the Trinity has been from the Greco-European perspective. I have noted earlier that theological interpretation is grounded in Cultural perspective. The theological interpretation of the Trinity as a model of God is always informed by the worldviews of the one engaged in the interpretative process. At the present moment a perspective is called for that will reclaim the influence of African worldview on the development of Christian theological thought. Such a perspective will need to provide a frame that is wholistic and reflects inclusiveness and justice, and respect for diversity. It is my conviction that the communal orientation of the African worldview applied to Divinity, particularly as developed in Tertullian's work on the Trinity, may offer such a perspective. The African understanding of the Divine is different from the Greco-European ideas that have dominated discussions about Divinity in modern thought systems. The fact is that theology, including liberation theologies, has been informed mostly by a modern western worldview, which makes an African perspective on this matter necessary. I believe that looking at the Trinity from an African perspective will contribute to the conversation.

NOTES

1. Joseph Bracken, Bracken *Society and Spirit* (Toronto: Associated University Press, 1991), 26.
2. Bracken, *Spirit and Society,* 27.
3. Ibid., 30.
4. Ibid., 104.
5. E. Bolaji Idowu, *African Traditional Religion: A Definition* (London: SCM Press, 1973), 103.
6. Ibid.
7. Immanuel Kant, *Der Streit der Fakultaten,* cited by Leonardo Boff in *Trinity and Society,* trans. Paul Burns (Maryknoll, N.Y.: Orbis Books, 1988), 19.
8. See Friedrich Schleiermacher, *The Christian Faith,* eds. H. R. MacKintosh and J. S. Stewart, trans. D. M. Baillie, et al. (Edinburgh: T. and T. Clark, 1928), 241, 738–39. This is in contrast to Karl Barth who complains that "Schleiermacher too could put the doctrines of the Trinity outside of the dogmatic *loci* and use it as a solemn conclusion to his whole dogmatic." For Barth "the fact that Schleiermacher can use the doctrine of the Trinity only as a conclusion to his dogmatics shows that it does not have constitutive significance for him." Karl Barth, *Church Dogmatics,* eds. Geoffrey W. Bromily and T. F. Torrance (Edinburgh: T. and T. Clark, 1975), 1:1.3031.
9. Schleiermacher, *The Christian Faith,* 739.
10. Friedrich Schleiermacher, *On the Discrepancy Between the Sabellian and Athanasian Method of Representing the Doctrine of the Trinity in the Godhead,* trans. M. Stuart (Andover, n.p. 1835), 145.

11. Barth, 1:1.3031.
12. Jürgen Moltmann, *The Trinity and the Kingdom,* trans. Margaret Kohl (San Francisco: Harper and Row, 1981), 1–2.
13. See William J. Hill, *The Three Personned God* (Washington, D.C.: Catholic University Press, 1982); and James P. Mackey, *The Christian Experience of God as Trinity* (London: SCM Press, 1983).
14. See Raimundo Pannikar, *The Trinity and the Religious Experience of Man* (Maryknoll, N.Y.: Orbis Books, 1973); and Ewert Cousins, "The Trinity and the World Religions," *Journal Of Ecumenical Studies* 7 (1970): 476–98.
15. Boff, 147–48.
16. Joseph Bracken, *Spirit and Society: A Trinitarian Cosmology* (London: Associated University Press, 1991)
17. Bracken, *Spirit and Society,* 70
18. Bracken, 123.
19. Ibid., 124.
20. Ibid.
21. Ibid., 69.
22. Bracken, *Society and Spirit* (Toronto: Associated University Press, 1991), 68.

One

TOWARD AN AFRICAN DEFINITION OF COMMUNITY

This chapter explores the definition of community. Communality is foundational to the African worldview. One finds this expressed in various ways in the thought and work of African scholars. Communality, relationality, and fundamental interconnection underlie the African mode of seeing and being in the world. The African pulse is continually "beating to communal rhythms and communal fears."[1] Indeed, "conscious cooperation in the community are among the highest values in the human being's existence—not separation, total independence, razor-edged competition and individuality for its own sake."[2] Community is a concept that is not so easily defined. Among Africans and non-Africans who write about African worldview, the concept of community is usually taken for granted. Kwesi Dickson noted that "it is commonplace that the sense of community is strong in Africa."[3] It is assumed that everyone knows what is meant by community. Furthermore, the philosophical or theological possibilities are supposed to be self-evident. Because of its importance for this discussion, I believe *community* needs definition to give the reader a feeling for how the term will be used.

I have chosen three authors with whom to interact so as to bring out a definition that reflects an African understanding of community. John Cobb and Herman Daly, in *The Common Good,* provide a working definition of community from an economic viewpoint. Ferdinand Toennies' seminal work, *Gemeinschaften und Gesellschaften,* provides a classical sociological definition of community. And Josiah Royce, in *The Problem of Christianity,* provides a philosophical definition. It is my contention that their definitions can contribute to the attempt to access the models of community inherent in various metaphoric ideas of the Divine that shall be discussed within this work.

DEFINITIONS OF COMMUNITY

John Cobb/Daly

John B. Cobb and Herman Daly, assume that community "does entail that membership in community contributes to self-identification."[4] They list three basic criteria that, for them, are definitive of authentic human community.

> A Society [community] should not be called a community unless (1) there is extensive participation by its members in the decision by which its life is governed, (2) the society [community] as a whole takes responsibility for the members, (3) this responsibility includes respect for the diverse individuality of its membership.[5]

Thus, participation, common responsibility, and respect for diverse individuality, are three criteria that determine genuine communality for Cobb and Daly.

These criteria, combined with the concept of openness, raise several issues regarding relationships: the relation of person and community, of freedom and participation, power and authority, equality and subordination. These issues will be used later to explore the conception of human relationality that corresponds with various conceptions of the Divine community.

Ferdinand Toennies

Since the publication of Ferdinand Toennies' *Community and Society (Gemeinschaft und Gesellschaft)*, a characteristic distinction has been made in scholarship between community and society.[6] In Toennies' work, *gemeinschaft* (community) has two characteristics. First, it is typically embodied in rural communities where personal relationships are characterized, explained, and guided by traditional rules. The second is that "simple and direct face-to-face relations with each other are determined by *Wesenswille* (natural-will) naturally and spontaneously arising expression of sentiments."[7] The problem with the second characteristic is that it lends itself easily to misinterpretation. The concentration on "direct face-to-face" relations fosters the belief that community is completely determined by physical or geographical Congruity Contiguity. This problem was made acute by the use of Toennies work after World War I, which led to the belief that community has been destroyed since people were no longer in continuous face-to-face relation.[8]

Community, however, must be more than a continuous face-to-face encounter. Toennies speaks of community as "relationships of mutual affirmation."[9] Either this is so, or one must exclude everyone who is geographically removed from the contiguity and tactility of community. It does seem, however, that mutual affirmation can occur even where there is distance between communal members.

Though Toennies does insist that the direct biological relational community is the real community, he does, however, refer to something called the "*Gemeinschaft* (Community) comprising all of [hu]mankind."[10] This community seems to extend the fundamental connection of human beings beyond that of immediate geographic proximity and immediate biology to include the natural connection of people everywhere.

This living community, is distinguished from what Toennies calls *Gesellschaft,* a gathering of people mechanically brought together, while being naturally unconnected, independent, and isolated from one another. To Toennies, then, genuine community is characterized by mutuality. Mutuality, then, will be used here to connote the idea of communal relations that includes the African idea of community and draws from Toennies' *Gemeinschaften,* which includes all humanity.

Josiah Royce

Josiah Royce has also contributed to the meaning of community. Royce's work, *The Problem of Christianity,* is one in which he offers valuable definitions of community. Indeed, the problem of Christianity is the problem of creating and maintaining a genuine universal community. This is not mainly the problem of Christianity but that of any genuine religious commitment to holisitic communal interaction. Royce contends that community means much more than social groups or natural groups. Royce defines community in a sense that it ceases from being restricted and exclusive, absorptive, or a mere aggregation of individuals. In Royce's opinion, community—that is, genuine community—is actual

> when many contemporary and distinct individual selves interpret each
> his own personal life, that each says of an individual past or of a
> determinate future event or deed: "that belongs to my life," "that
> occurred or will occur to me," then these many selves may be defined

as hereby constituting, in a perfectly definite and objective, but also highly significant, sense, a community.[11]

For Royce, people may be said to constitute a community with reference to that particular past or future event, or group of events, which each accepts or interprets as belonging to one's past or to one's individual future.[12] This coming together is made possible by the fact that these individuals have been connected by the Spirit or what can be referred to as common human nature. In light of African worldview, this connection might be referred to as "preter-connection," a connection that happens before the fact of contiguous gathering. Community is made of people who share a past and future together in Spirit, which serves as an integrative principle. This sharing can happen even in the absence of a constant direct face-to-face encounter or even immediate biological connection. The past, as a matter of fact, is replete with persons and things of which the individual knows absolutely nothing in terms of Physical rapprochement. This may be the idea behind the use of such terms as extended family. Indeed, the African family is a community that extends itself beyond even those whom we remember or with whom we are conscious of being connected. Royce's perspective is sometimes very compatible with an African perspective, particularly when he states that community consists of "many individuals in one spiritual bond."[13]

The African conception of communality, particularly as manifested among the Igbos of West Africa, consists of a spiritual unity that binds people together, thus creating a communal bond that is unbreakable by distance or death.

Royce also distinguishes between "natural community" and "genuine community," which he refers to as "the Beloved Community" based on the nature of love manifested in both.[14] The natural community leads so easily to exclusivism, sinful control, and other "arts of spiritual hatred."[15] The dangers in the overemphasis of "natural community" is quite evident in Africa. One has merely to take a casual glance to see the "sinfulness" of tribalistic mentality in African nations. But that possibility by itself does not mean that "natural community" is sinful merely by being such. On the other hand, in Royce's work one also finds what he connotes a genuine community. Frank Oppenheim, commenting on what Royce regards as a genuine community, notes:

[The genuine community] is one in which a living conscious union of love and loyalty binds members to each other and to their community and it to him. In it members have been transformed from being "lost individuals" into such wholehearted servants of the community that they are opened to universal loyalty towards all minded beings and to the growth of universal loyalty to everyone.[16]

For Royce, whatever this genuine community represented, the natural community represented its distorted and demonic counterpart.[17]

The question that Royce's treatment raises is this: Is a genuine or universal community possible without a natural community? Royce seems to think so. Africa is a clear example of the problem of the natural community that Royce raises. But I want to insist that the natural community—which is the natural connection of human beings, which is by nature an unsolicited, unlabored for, fundamental belonging of the human being—is, nonetheless, the genuine ground for whatever universally genuine community is possible. It does not seem that a people who have lost the sense of natural community can build a genuinely universal community. Without this basic communal interconnection, it is virtually impossible to build community. The genuine community then, is the result of the universalizing of the feelings of relatedness and belonging that are within the natural community; this is done through various transformative procedures. Such transformative procedures in African religious settings are embodied in rituals, such as the rituals of initiation into various stages or dimensions of life. While exclusivism may result from the natural community, within the natural community is the possibility for an open, transforming and genuine universal community.

For Royce, one connecting principle for the human community is interpretation. The act of interpretation proceeds in triadic concentricity, in which the community is a sign needing interpretation, the presence of an interpreter and the audience (the-willing-to-be-interpreted-to). The community for Royce is semiotic.[18] In discussing Community then, the semiotic principle of sign function is key for Royce. Semiotic is the interpretive process by which Community attains Self-definition. The interpretation Process connects the members, helps them criticize, and help them create newness within Community.

One problem remains in Royce's concept of Community. Royce does not deal with the question of the status of those members of community who cannot grasp or act according to this purely rationalistic interpretative process. Neither does he recognize that interpretation presupposes community and belonging. Where no natural communal connection is presupposed, what will be present, even in terms of Royce's and Toennies's definitions of community, will be an aggregation of externally tangential persons. As such, then, interpretation is not the basis or the condition for being in community, though it may serve instrumentally for its preservation and perpetuation.

From an African-centered perspective Community and Interpretation can best be seen in terms of levels of activity. The experience of belonging is a primary activity. Belonging precedes ratiocinative interpretative processes. Interpretation is a secondary level of communal activity. It is very important to place interpretation within community, within the locus of that spiritual connection and relation upon which any humane discourse must be grounded. It underscores the idea of the principle of participation and realizing that interpretation is not foundational to Communal belonging raises the problem of freedom as part of the Concept of Community. Interpretation presupposes the idea of freedom, as freedom presupposes personality within Community. Interpretation, then, rightly belongs to the activity that is carried on within community.

Another principle that serves the purpose of communal connectivity and undergirds genuine communality for Royce is the concept of loyalty. Loyalty serves to undergird the interplay of the person and community.

Another key concept affects Royce's definition of a genuine community is that of time or the temporal process. Temporality is a communal problem, be it temporality of the gods or of humanity who emulates the gods. Royce shows that the temporal process is what helps the evolution of community. Explaining this effect of the time process, Royce states:

> [A] true community is essentially a product of the time process. A community has a past and will have a future. Its more or less conscious history, real or ideal, is a part of its essence. A community requires for its existence a history and is greatly aided by its conscious memory.[19]

Royce also draws an analogy between the impact of time process in personal growth and the transformative effect of the time process on the community. For example, in spite of the various activities of the person, a human being is considered a unity. This idea is transferred analogously to the community. This is Royce's way of clarifying and supporting his idea that the communal structures and processes are subject to historical changes. He states,

> The rule that time is needed for the formation of a conscious community is a rule which finds its extremely familiar analogy within the life of every individual human self. Each one of us knows that he just now, at this instant, cannot find more than a fragment of himself present. The self comes down to us from the past. It needs a history.[20]

The memory, which is formed by the time process, may work either to preserve familiar structures that may be oppressive or for the dissolution of the familiar structures. Not only does time help the building of community, but it does so sometimes by rendering the communal structures changeable. In the latter case, the memories that have been accumulated through time can become dangerous to existing structures. Hence, the concept of the temporality of functional structures must then be seen as a criterion for what is to be considered a genuine community, because it assures an openness to change.

Summary

Now to recapitulate what has been said above. From Cobb and Daly, the criteria of participation and respect for personhood have been gleaned. These criteria will be used to explore various modes of communal relationality that correspond with various conceptions of the Divine community. In doing this, the concept of openness shall be kept in mind as well. From Toennies comes the idea that genuine community is characterized by mutuality. Royce's definition of community also provides certain key concepts that will be helpful in considering the various models of human community. Among these concepts are belonging and interpretation. Belonging is a concept which, for Royce, is informed by one's participation in the past and future of the community. Interpretation is a secondary activity of community, and it presupposes community, it also allow for distinctive personalities within the community, and allows persons to participate in freedom. These ideas themselves are helpful for the discussion of models of human community.

AN AFRICAN DEFINITION OF COMMUNITY

For the African, a fundamental philosophical assumption is that face-to-face encounter is vital for community, but the existence and perpetuation of community depends on more than actual physical encounter; spiritual ties to the community always exist. Of course, the African communal orientation tends to be based squarely on tribal loyalty. Yet, the African metaphysical orientation demands that community be more than a physical face-to-faceness.

> In the context of Africa, people are surrounded not by things but by beings—the metaphysical world is loaded with beings. Thinking in this context is synthetic rather than analytically oriented, which implies that everything is interdependent and in the end has religious value. The traditional approach does not have place for something religiously neutral. Furthermore, the whole of reality is of primary concern. Nature is not objectified as in science; orientation towards totality is reflected in the intense feeling of community. In modernist thinking, the principle of identity prevails—there is no sharing of being. For the traditional person in Africa, a communal unity of essence is possible—an individual is never a mere individual, but is also the other (who is also another).[21]

Community in African contexts include the precarnate, the carnate, and the discarnate.[22] Jean Marc Ela contends that African ancestors should be included in the community of the saints.[23] This insistence, which seems pervasive among African scholars, underscores the idea of community. It is a community that reaches into the past, respects the present, and anticipates the future in the gods and the ancestors. The African feels a sense of loyalty to community that transcends the geographical boundaries, so much so that when a person is in a different geographical location he or she is not considered out of community. The idea of leaving one's community is, in a sense, meaningless as one always carries with him or her the community. From this perspective it is, therefore, impossible to destroy community because genuine communality is based on a *common union,* a union grounded on the fact that humanity shares a common nature (a nature that was neither created by human beings, nor can it be destroyed by them) that connects them to one another. The issue then is not whether we shall have community or not, but how people are related to one another in community and how this relation is legitimized.

In African worldview, mutual relation is far more than a dyadic relation in which two are lost uncritically in each other. The African emphasis on offspring assures that dyadic relation does not lead to egotism can be avoided because there is always the possibility of a "third presence." The idea of mutuality means that "every such relationship represents unity and plurality or plurality in unity."[24]

An African idea of community sees openness as its fundamental principle. Understandably, openness is not given prominence in Cobb and Daly's work because of its emphasis on economics. Such an economic definition of community is definitely not beyond criticism particularly from the perspective of this person-oriented communal concept of Africa. From an African perspective, one more explicit criterion should added to the criteria developed by Cobb and Daly, that of *openness.*

Openness is and must be a criterion in defining both human and Divine community. The openness proposed here is two-pronged. One prong is directed within the community and the other without. Such openness must have both horizontal and vertical dimensions. The community that is genuinely called community is capable of being open to newness that springs from within itself, as well as that which emerges from the periphery and outside of the community. It needs to be admitted, however, that there is no such thing as absolute openness to those on the periphery.

For much of what has been said regarding Royce's concept of community, comparable concepts of community can also be found within African worldviews. African worldview see everything as embodiment of spirit. Community is connected by the fact of what might be termed *spiritness,* which is shared by all and in which all participate. This spiritness assures distinction and connection within any given community. Members of community share in one power, yet because of the unique expression of spirit in each person this power allows each member an exercise of freedom. This freedom might lead persons to take a variety of roles in the community, to experiment with his or her uniqueness and connection to the whole.

Historical experiments undertaken by persons, because of their uniqueness serves to transform the community. For the contribution of the person to be effective, the community must be open to new possibilities—to creativity and generativity. The measure of authentic community lies partly in the adequacy of the patterns of human communal interactions within it.

Community is not just a state but a process of being in the world—a process that includes the past, the present, and the future.

The problem for African theologians has been the claim by missionaries and theologians that theological understanding is an immediate result of God's self-revelation unaffected by the intellectual orientation or the cultural biases of those who came to Africa to communicate this Supernatural self-revelation of God to them. Until recently, even African theologians seem to have worked from this assumption that somehow there is an objective revelative theological insight independent of the human structuring of, and interaction, with reality. But revelation happens within Community. "Community is not merely and ultimate ideal, it is also an immediate necessity."[25] Thus revelative "Persuasion is power mixed within a particular mode of communality."[26] Revelation as inherent within "communality is radical because it is interpersonal openness maintained in opposition to social impersonality."[27]

> A community exists when the experience of personal interdependence is the basis of relation within the community. The bond of community exist where a person is taken as person and allowed to relate on the basis of fundamental belonging within their referential totality.[28]

Within various African contexts religion functions as the basis for self-transcendence, a capacity that is originally developed in intimate community. Religion as a communal principle may finally attain to "cosmic consciousness," because it begins with the immediate ties of love that are so important to Africans. Hence, it naturally uses the language of the face-to-face community to speak of love, fellowship, brotherhood, communion, fatherhood of God.[29] These concepts are not graspable, really, until one looks at the primal and tribal mode of being in the world, which in itself is highly experiential.

From the African point of view "everything in creation and indeed the universe as a whole exhibits a basic structure of existence and activity which is ordered to community."[30] The idea of personal interconnection within community is foundational to a theological understanding of God.

An African concept of community holds the individual and the community in balance. While the individuals are essential in and of themselves for the generative continuation of a world, "community as an ontological reality is in some sense superior to its person-members and can be described properly by philosophical categories, provided that one choose carefully those categories."[31] A community, cannot and should not be reduced to a Hobsian "network of relations between separate individuals who are first and foremost themselves and only secondly placed within association with one another."[32] Such conceptualization of community makes it seem as though the individual is prior to community, there are individuals first before there is community. Within an African framework, individuals are not "themselves" and then, second, placed within community. If this is what Bracken means then he is also committing the error that lays the foundation for separating the individual from the community. The individual is primarily connected to others psychically, spiritually, and physically, and second, a "for-her/himself" individual. Even in one's individuality one is never truly separated from his or her fundamental communal connection. Unless one sees this connection of persons as radical and fundamental, one is likely to run the risk of the false separation that has characterized much of philosophical thought in the West and has contributed to the obfuscation of the doctrine of the Trinity.

NOTES

1. Victor Taylor, *The Primal Vision* (London: SCM Press, 1963), 35.
2. Osthuzien, 45; Friday M. Mbon, "African Traditional Socio-Religious Ethics and National Development" in *African Traditional Religions in Contemporary Society* ed., Jacob K. Olupona (New York: Paragon House, 1991),
3. See Dickson, *Theology in Africa* (Maryknoll, N. Y.: Orbis Books, 1984), 62.
4. Herman E. Daly and John B. Cobb, *For the Common Good* (Boston: Beacon Press, 1989), 172.
5. Ibid.
6. Ferdinand Toennies, *Community and Society (Gemeinschaft und Gesellschaft)*, trans. Charles P. Loomis (East Lansing: Michigan State University Press, 1957), 12.
7. "Gemeinschaft and Gesellschaft," *Encyclopedia Britannica*, 15th ed.
8. Ibid.
9. Toennies, 33.
10. Ibid.
11. Josiah Royce, *The Problem of Christianity* (Chicago: University of Chicago Press, 1968), 248. See also Frank Oppenheim, *Royce's Mature Philosophy of Religion* (Notre Dame, Ind.: University of Notre Dame Press, 1987), 29.
12. Ibid.
13. Royce, *The Problem of Christianity*, 133.
14. Ibid., 129 and 130.
15. Royce, *The Problem of Christianity*, 131.
16. Oppenheim, 29.
17. Royce, *The Problem of Christianity*, 129.
18. Royce, *The Problem of Christianity*, 340. The section titled, "The Doctrine of Signs," 345–51.
19. Royce, *The Problem of Christianity*, 243.
20. Royce, *The Problem of Christianity*, 244.
21. Gerhardus Cornelis Oosthuizen, "The Place of Traditional Religion in Contemporary South Africa," in ed., Jacob K. Olupona *African Traditional Religion in Contemporary Society* (New York: Paragon House, 1991) 40–41.
22. African community includes the living dead and, in some settings those who are not yet physically born. See John Mbiti, *African Religion and Philosophy* (New York: Praeger, 1969).

23. See Ela, *My Faith as an African.* trans. John P. Brown and Susan Perry (Maryknoll, N.Y.: Orbis Books, 1988).

24. Ibid.

25. Glen Tinder, *The Political Meaning of Christianity* (Baton Rouge: Louisiana State University, 1989), 160.

26. Ibid., 161.

27. Ibid., 204.

28. Melvin Rader, *Ethics and the Human Community* (New York: Holt, Rinehart and Winston, 1964).

29. Ibid., 411.

30. Ibid., 7.

31. Ibid., 19.

32. Ibid.

Two

AFRICAN DIVINITY:
A COMMUNAL DEFINITION

Communality is the essence of the gods.[1]

The debate regarding the problem of the One and the Many is relevant to Africa today. Within African Scholarship the debate has to do with the nature of the African Concept of God. The question in African scholarship has been whether African traditional religion conceives of the Divine as an absolute, singular, personalistic God (monotheism) or whether it is conceived of in separatistic (polytheistic) terms. The latter view assumes many gods with completely separate natures, unconnected and not intrinsically related. This is what Tertullian seems to have been rejecting when he rejected Marcion's proposal of two Divine natures at odds with each other. For this type we shall reserve the term *polytheism.*

In the debate about the nature of the Concept of God in Africa, two major positions can be delineated, that of monotheism and polytheism or separatistic theism. The second strand usually refered to as *polytheistic,* I refer to as separationist, creates confusion when it is used in reference to an African conception of Divinity. Polytheism at least as used in reference to Africa has become a pejorative term that fails to take account of the fundamentality of relationship within the Divine. Hence, the term *polytheism* will be used here to refer not only to many gods, but to separatism among the gods. The form of pluralism that appears in the African context and has a positive valuation of diversity within the Divine will be described by the term *community* and its derivatives.

While it is true that there are two predominant positions in the debate, I believe there is a third option. The first position deals with monotheism, the second deals with polytheism, and the third deals with the Divine conceived as a community of gods. In my opinion African scholars have

failed to recognize this last possibility. This is a serious fault since communality is central to the way in which most, if not all, Africans understand
the world.

The centrality of communality underscores the fundamental and irrevo-
cable belief of the African in relationality. For the African, everyone, and
in fact everything in the world, is related—connected by an all-pervasive
force. As John S. Mbiti puts it, "each individual is a brother-in-law, uncle
or aunt, or something else to everybody else. That means that everybody
is related to everybody else."[2] However, relatedness is not primarily
between so-called rational beings. This relatedness is inclusive of the
whole cosmos. This profound sense of relatedness in African contexts is
the ground of Mbiti's aphorism, "I am because we are, and since we are,
therefore I am," or in its populist version, "I belong, therefore I am."[3]
Attempting to understand the Divine from this point of view leads me to
conclude that the Divine in the African context is a community of gods,*
or in Tertullian's terms, a community of persons. The centrality of community and the fundamentality of relatedness undergird the concept of the
Divine as community in African contexts. But some monotheists and
polytheists will disagree with this, so consideration of these views will
provide a fuller picture.

MONOTHEISTIC STRAND

In the debate about the Divine in Africa, the monotheistic strand has
figured prominently. It is that strand within the debate about God that
insists that the traditional African believes in one singular and personal
God.

The idea that African traditional religions are monotheistic in nature
has been very strong in African scholarly thought since the 1930s. I
believe that African scholars have taken the western theologians too
seriously in their understanding of God as an absolute, universal, personalistic principle, or as H. Richard Niebuhr calls radical monotheism.[4] There
is no such monotheistic radicality in African traditional religions. Those
African scholars who, like their Western partners, have proposed that
African religion is characterized by monotheism are not wholly correct.
For such scholars, monotheism means an absolute, personalistic God.

---

* This term is used deliberately so as not to obscure the divine nature of African gods.
It should also be remembered that the problem of God with Capital G and gods with
small letters is an English linguistic problem and has become an African problem mainly
by imposition.

These African scholars do not hesitate to equate the so-called High God or great God with a personal monotheistic conception of deity.[5]

In fact, various African peoples do refer to the deity in personal terms and with personal names. Whether this implies a single personality will depend on two criteria: (1) that such a name refers only to the one entity and under no circumstance should such a name refer to any other; and (2) that such a one be completely alone in its class without another who is remotely capable of sharing the same nature with it. But, if the traditional Africans use similar language or names to refer to other objects/subjects, or if there are entities that may remotely be seen as other gods related to the so-called supreme God, then any proposal for African monotheism is problematic.

Many African scholars are bent on proving the existence of an absolute monotheism of a singular personalistic deity in African traditional religions. Some like E. Bolaji Idowu, for example, have sometimes dealt with the problem of the One and Many by creating an arbitrary distinction between what they call the divinities and deity proper.[6] The emphasis on monotheism was due mainly to a reaction to the negative evaluations of African religion and worldview by scholars of the so-called major religions.

But the distinction between Divinity and deity as a way of substantiating African monotheism is replete with problems. Many nagging questions are raised by this distinction. For example, what is the validity of this distinction in the African context, particularly since gods are necessarily Divine? Idowu deals with the problem by positing a supreme God, who is ontologically separate from other divinities. He refers to this God as Deity. How consistent with African philosophy of wholeness and fundamental relationality is this separation? One may ask: If the so-called supreme God is not Divine while the other gods are Divine, should the supreme God even be called God at all? How can that which is not Divine be God at all? The separation between the great God and the other gods, if it is meant to show that there is only one God, is arbitrary and in fact misleading.

Even if one were to accept this distinction, is one obliged to maintain that this proves monotheism in the case of African religion? Also, how is one to account for the dynamic orientation of African religion? Is it not in the belief that one principle pervades and multiplies in all the gods? The concept of vital force—*Ntu* among the Bantu, *Suman* among the Ashanti, *Chi* or ndu[7] among the Igbos—seems to point to a nonpersonalistic principle to which prefixes or suffixes are added to denote personality in the process of becoming.[8] This fundamental principle is neutral with regard to personality. The principle is all-pervasive in itself and has the potential for creative and generative diversification. All these questions and more arise as one discusses the concept of the One and the Many in African traditional religions. All the questions raised above point to some basic problems inherent in any position that intends to argue for an African monotheism. Kwesi Dickson has pointed out that "there is no easy solution to the problem of the relation between God and the gods."[9] As Dickson sees the issue, the categories of monotheism and polytheism obfuscates rather than clarifies the discussion. However, my contention is that it is not the relation that is problematic, but the refusal of African scholars to use African communal categories for their Divination. An African Monotheism is a philosophical oxymoron. The problem is the categorial fallacy into which Africans have been led by the colonial language.

Joseph B. Danquah, one of the pioneers in the study of African doctrines of God, argues forcefully for the oneness of God. Danquah describes God among the Akan of Ghana as "the great ancestor."[10] Danquah uses a nomological approach to the study of belief in God.[11] He maintains that a people's understanding of God is to be found in the name they give to God. It follows, for him, that the names that the Akan give such a being summarize their belief. He proceeds to state emphatically that "names reveal which God is the true God."[12] Such an approach, while having possibilities, is replete with problems. The possibilities emerge from the significance of names in African cultures. Names among the Igbos, for example, convey the deepest feeling of those who name, and they sometimes describe the characteristics of the named. But even if one concurred with such a traditional African understanding of names and their power, the idea that the name of the Supreme Being refers to one superior person is problematic. The same names may be used for other beings. And if the logic is followed, those beings who somehow manage to share the same name should be seen as being the same with the Supreme Being both in nature and power.

Another implication is that names change, even names of the deity. In Africa some names are determined by experiences and as new experiences emerge, these names may change. In fact, even the possibility of misnaming and lying is always present in names. Names seem not to reveal the true God, but rather to reveal what we think the characteristic of any true god should be. The human understanding of what a true god should be is not static and unchangeable.

Danquah recognizes this multiple use of names in his discussion of the Akan usage of *Nana*. The term *Nana* is a title often used to refer to the so-called supreme God, but it also denotes any prestigious persons within the Akan society, particularly an elder.[13] Another good example of the problem inherent in this nomological approach is the use of the name *Mulungu*. Danquah translates the word variously, "the old one" or "great one," intending by this translation to support the so-called African monotheism.[14]

Edwin Smith, on the other hand, contends that the word does not represent personality. Rather, according to Smith, Mulungu

> sums up at once the creative energy which made the earth and animals and man [*sic*] and powers which operate in human life. . . . it is sometimes considered as spirit within; sometimes regarded as a universal agency in native affairs impalpable, impersonal; sometimes rising into distinctness as god.[15]

To add to the problem, Carl Meinhorf, in his work, derives the word *Mulungu* from the Bantu word *Lungu,* which means clan family.[16] Since Meinhorf was the first to study the meaning of this word, it is most likely that he possessed the traditional meaning of the term. *Lungu* is still used among some Bantus to refer to the people of the clan. *Mulungu,* in all likelihood, therefore, did not stand for a singular personal God, but to a clan of gods.

From the study of Akan names for God, Danquah concludes that God is the great ancestor and this certifies the singularity of God. At one point in his work, Danquah contends:

> The Akan doctrine of God teaches that He is the great ancestor. He [*sic*] is a true high God and manlike ancestor. He [*sic*] deserves to be worshipped and is worshipped in the visible ancestral head, the good chief of the community.[17]

For Danquah this ancestor is "singular and eternal" and only differentiated in name, not in reality.[18] Another problem raised by Danquah's discussion of the Akan doctrine of God concerns his admission that other gods in the Akan history may have been regarded as the great god until they were displaced by *Onyankopon* "the greater Nyame." If some god other than *Nyame* has ever been considered supreme, then one is no longer talking about one singular, supreme god for all times. Even the concept of one singular ancestor loses its force as an argument for monotheism.

The Igbo word *Chukwu,* which means "great god," has been used as proof of African monotheism. But this word is not necessarily a reference to one singular deity. Sometimes the so-called minor gods are referred to in terms that describe them as great gods. The greatness of any particular god depends on the experience of the individual addressing the God. For example, a diviner/prophet prays, *"Amadi oha Chukwu aka mu di kwa ocha"* (Amadi Oha, great god, my hands are clean). *Amadi Oha* is the god of justice and is here identified with *Chukwu* or Great God. Amadi Oha is the god of justice. This god carries out the sentences of the gods. The symbols of this god are thunder and lightning. Lightening is often interpreted wrongly as being a symbol of anger, but this is not necessarily accurate. In the Igbo land where night storms are common, which makes the night seem darker, the lightning is the only light, and its flashing helps one to see where one is going more clearly. I have heard elders in the midst of a storm at night (when coming home from the farm) say, *"Amadi oha chi ukwu ekene mu gi"* (Amadi Oha, great god, I greet or thank you) giving thanks for the light that the lightning brings to illuminate their way.

In a situation where justice needs to be done to right injustices, it is not anger as such that determines the striking of the thunder and lightning on the unjust individual, but the words that the individual utters during the trial in the presence of the community. For example, people say, "If I have done this injustice, may Amadi Oha not protect me, rather may I be struck by you." In this sense it is the words of the individual that determine the striking out, not because Amadi Oha is angry with the person. The individuals, if they suffer, do so because of their refusal to accept and make reparation for injustices.

Among the Igbo people, the concept of *Chukwu* is a term that can refer to the gods as one mighty community, to particular gods who have performed particular functions that are considered by the individual worshiper to be great. Monotheism is not necessarily implied by the names "supreme god," "most high god," "father of all," and of course, "great ancestor."

At one point in his discussion, Danquah concedes that even among the Akan the name "Nyame, . . . is reserved for spirit gods or god who is supreme."[19] The term *great* points to a hierarchy of functions, especially since most of the terms tend toward social distribution of responsibility, not necessarily based on an inherent ontologically superior personal God. Sometimes Danquah seems to imply that the name of God is unchangeable, at other times he concedes that the name does not necessarily refer to one supreme God. This underscores the problem of using name/s as a way to prove African monotheism.

Scholars of Bantu languages inform us that the references to personality within the language do not denote an abstract concept of personhood, which lends itself easily to individualism. The concept of person among the Bantu, as with other African people, is dynamic. This dynamic understanding of personhood has been expressed philosophically in the word *Ntu,* which represents the concept of a vital universal force, a dynamic power that is embodied in all being and is all pervasive.[20] Scholars of African religion have to face the problem created by the English word "god" and the arbitrary distinction between God and gods. This distinction forces African scholars to make distinctions such as the one made between divinities and deity; this results in a relegation of at least some of the gods of the African people to a non-god or an ontologically subordinate status. Having opted for personal monotheism, one is limited in understanding how the gods with lower-case "g" are related with the God of the upper-case "G." Does the use of the upper case "G" imply *primus inter pares* (first among equals), or the existence of only one personal God with no equals, or no communal members possessing the same nature as the High God? If one assumes that all gods cannot be called God, one will need to explain how such phrases as the "supreme God," "the most high God," and "the Father of the gods" are to be interpreted in light of the presence of all other deities, some of which even the monotheists concede are considered direct descendants of the so-called supreme God.

The problem is accentuated by unclear statements about African monotheism sometimes found in the work of Mbiti and Idowu. The fact that Africans speak of a great God is taken to imply monotheism according to Mbiti. He then proceeds to discuss the attributes of this Divine being as though they belong to one singular personal being.[21] But there is no sociological or logical necessity in the culture of traditional African religionists for the assumption that the attributes must belong to one individual god. These are theological decisions made by some scholars to make Africa fit, in spite of its cultural difference.[22] In various African contexts, the other gods share in these Divine attributes. When one looks at this from the perspective that the Divine is a community, one may come to see that the community is the one possessing these attributes.

Danquah is very insightful in regards to this point. While maintaining his theory of the Divine as ancestor, he cautions against defining the omnipotence of God in individualistic terms. Danquah indicates that

> the omnipotence of the high-father is conditioned by the fact that he is the great ancestor or begetter of the life of the community and of those who participate in it.[23]

For Danquah, grounding the attribute omnipotence in community affords a "solution which is final, but the prevailing popular conception in Western Europe is that the high-father or the High One is absolute Omnipotence, a monarch absolute in his [sic] own right."[24] The idea of the omnipotence of the high-father in Danquah's opinion, "cannot be greater than the reality of community."[25] The logical necessity on the part of traditional Africans will be to suppose that whichever god is supreme, it is one member of a family of gods. A god incapable of having children or incapable of being in close familial relationship is not truly god; a god incapable of working within a community of beings of similar substance would be highly suspect.

This monotheistic orientation in African scholarship has gone so far as to deny the common African worldview, that is, the presence of kinship through progeny (even among the gods) and the basic communal interconnection within the Divine. In Mbiti's pioneering work *Concepts of God in Africa,* for example, he appears to trivialize the communality of the Divine in Africa by maintaining that the concept of a wife of God "is more of a logical necessity than a serious conviction, springing from the social structure which makes it more convenient to give God a wife than to think of him as having none."[26] If, in fact, it is a logical necessity, it is a necessity that springs from the deep African conviction that to be alone is to be cursed. Hence, in traditional African thought, God cannot be one (alone), *Unus,* in the sense of singular; God must be communal. A people's experience of social necessity is built into their logic of being-in-the-world; it speaks to what is real for them as well as what is possible in the realm of thought. The African conception of a wife for any god is real and necessary. To trivialize this concept, as Mbiti does, is to ignore the pivotal importance of communality in African worldview. Even analogically speaking, the idea of Divine progeny leads not to monotheism but to a plurality of gods.

E. Bolaji, who has written one of the definitive works about African traditional religion, also insists on the monotheism of African traditional religion. Idowu tempers this monotheistic tendency by speaking of a diffused monotheism. Idowu asserts:

> I do not know any place in Africa where the ultimacy is not accorded to God. That is why, because this is very true of the Yoruba, I conclude that the religion can only be adequately described as monotheistic. I modify this "monotheism" by the adjective "diffused," because here there exist other powers which derive from Deity such being and authority that they can be treated, for all practical purposes, almost as ends in themselves.[27]

If this monotheism is diffused, and there are indeed other gods who share in the power of the Divine and may be treated as ends in themselves, this cannot really be called monotheism in the most limited sense.

It appears that Idowu recognizes the problem of claiming monotheism for African religion when he complains of "priestcrafts."* However he speaks of one Deity, it needs to be seen as the summation of the nature that pervades the gods, and it is their power as a community of beings; it is not one person. This one is a *one* that is also *many*; within the One is plurality. If the monotheism is diffused, then it can no longer be called *mono* in the sense of one person.

SEPARATIONISTIC POLYTHEISM STRAND

The presence of numerous gods is also recognized in African scholarship, but mostly in the negative sense. The polytheism that concerns us here is that which separates the Divine nature into many disparate parts. One major example of the idea of fundamental dualism is manifested in the thought of Marcion. The term polytheism itself has become pejorative and value-laden. In the western mind, the term connotes an inferior concept of the Divine. It is regarded as the bastion of superstitions, even by Africans. This understandably has created an African reaction against the use of the word polytheism in the African context.

---

* This is a term used by E. Bolaji Idowu to refer to the exploitation of people by priests through religious ideology.

Both African and foreign scholars recognize this, and most share the negative attitude. For example, Danquah calls all things that do not deal with god in monotheistic form superstitions. His words deserve to be quoted here: "Akan religious doctrine knows only one God. Everything else found in the land in the form of religion is nothing else but superstition."[28] Idowu indicts this conception of gods in Africa for perpetuating of what he calls "priestcraft," meaning the ideological, oppressive manipulation which he maintains often attends the worship of these gods.[29]

Though Danquah and other Africans may disagree with my interpretation, I think that Danquah recognizes the plurality of gods when he states that "if a people center the good around the family and community, they are bound to consider God (the ideal of a chief good) as being the head of a family." Danquah, at one point in his discourse on God, acknowledges that the monotheism of which he speaks is "implicit in Nyame."[30] Therefore, if the term is implicit and not explicit, then both the term *family* and the implicitness of which Danquah speaks point to the fact that there is a plurality of gods in the African concept of the Divine. It follows, then, that if one accepts the term polytheism in the Africa context, such acceptance would not be separatistic. Rather, it could mean the acceptance of and loyalty to many centers without necessarily feeling a sense of conflict among the centers. The belief in many gods without seeing the need to have one of them considered ontologically superior to the others is what characterizes a communal conception of the Divine.

But, if one accepts that God is singular rather than communal, then any sharing and multiplication could be seen as necessitating a division within the Divine, leading to conflict and complete separation of natures. Herein lies the fear that the concept of polytheism strikes at the heart of monotheism, although it has been stated that polytheism does not necessarily mean Divine antagonism. The conceptual problem is real, however, because the presence of Divine separation is not completely absent from history. However, Divine separationism is virtually absent from African theologies of the Divine. This absence may explain the intensity with which African scholars reject the polytheism concept. At least to the present moment, African scholars have not suggested separationism as an African concept of the Divine. This does not mean that scholars deny the idea of distinctive, and sometimes hierarchical, responsibility within community. They deny, instead, a hierarchy of nature within the Divine community.

Though the African religious scholars who have been considered in this discussion advocate monotheism, there is a tension in their work that shows that they are aware of the pluralistic orientation of the African concept of the Divine. This tension is found in Danquah's emphasis on the Divine as the head of a community or family and in Idowu's acceptance of the idea of a diffused monotheism.

DIVINE COMMUNALISM: A THIRD STRAND

Danquah and Idowu's emphasis on monotheism seem to be tempered by an acknowledgment of plurality, but they fail to do full justice to an African concept of the Divine. The reason for this failure is due partly to the inadequacy of the categories of monotheism and polytheism that they used to explain African thought about the Divine. This discussion proposes a third category—the Divine as community—as a more adequate way of conceiving and explaining Divinity in African contexts. Divine Communalism is the position that the Divine is a community of gods who are fundamentally related to one another and ontologically equal while at the same time distinct from one another by their personhood and functions.

African worldview is characterized by the socioreligious factor of imma-nent communality and the time-and-distance-transcending concepts of relationality. The term *immanent* refers to the fact that relationality is seen as an intrinsic part of being in the world. Transcendence refers to the fact that such a concept of relationality (as well as its actuality) is incapable of being fettered by geographic distance or physiological de-carnation (death). Speaking with regard to African relationality, Mbiti states: "The individual is united with the rest of his community, both the living and the dead, and humanly speaking nothing can separate [the person] from this corporate [community]."[31] Even divinely speaking, the human being cannot be separated as traditional Africans never spoke of eternal punish-ment.

In many parts of Africa, being single and alone is the one perennially repeated curse. For example, the Igbo have considered it such a curse that until modern times, they did not bury a person who was single. Reproduction or generation, which is the diversification and pluralizing of nature, is considered a blessing and an improvement on singleness.[32] Thus, the lack of progeny is considered a great tragedy. This sociological value for African peoples is ignored by the monotheistic propagators who see some merit in arguing for one personal God. The emphasis on generativity also underscores the importance of the process of becoming in African contexts. The process is applicable to the Divine as well as to other modes of being in the universe.

The Igbo word *Chukwu,* often used as proof of African monotheism, is misleading. The word is a combination of the Igbo word *Chi* as prefix and the suffix *Ukwu* (great). The combination results in *Chukwu* (the great god). When the suffix *Na 'eke* (to be creating) is added to *Chi* the result is the name *Chineke* (God, the creating one). All of these combinations have been used as an argument for personalistic monotheism.[33] But if this God is seen as person in various African contexts, it is one among many, not one ontologically superior personality separated from all other gods.

As for creativity, there is hardly a god among the Igbo that is not creative in some sense. Each one of the gods was involved in the creation of the world and continues to be involved in the creative processes within the universe. For example, the earth Goddess *Ani* (with the variations *Ana, Ale, Ala*) is one without whom there will be no creation on earth as we see it, including human beings. *Ani* prepares a place of rest for the ancestors who have gone to the netherworld. So, *Ani* is *Chi.* And in fact for those who worship *Ani,* there is no reason why *Ani* should not be *Chukwu* (great god). Illogu maintains that "Ala the earth goddess, is the most important deity in Ibo social life. She is the guardian of morality, the controller of the minor gods of fortune and economic life. . . ."[34] However, as has been previously noted, the concept *Chi* (without the suffixes), like the word *Lungu,* refers not to a person or personalized god, but to a particular kind of force that, when personified, is equivalent to what is considered god. At most, the term refers to gods in general. Sometimes in the Igbo language the term is used as a name for a person's tutelary deity or spiritual double who guards the person through life. This possible confusion not withstanding, *Chi* is the term for any Divine being.

So a god is a Divine person and, as a Divine person, is not the whole Divinity. This personification is not one but many. Manyness is not in opposition to the concept of oneness, but it is inclusive of all of the gods. To claim that only one can be Divine is similar to the claim that because a village has a chief who is a man, there must be only one real man in the village instead of seeing the chief as one man among many men. It is also similar to claiming that the chief is the only human being, because he or she represents society at a particular point in history. So capital letter or not, in the African traditional religion, a god is a god, is a god, is a God. A god does not cease to be of the same nature with other gods even if that god has been chosen to represent the rest. It is precisely because a god shares in the same nature as all of the other beings that warrants it being called god. One god is inextricably related to the other gods by virtue of the Divine nature.

The presence of family, generativity, and proliferation among the gods points to the presence in African religious thought of both the concept of the One (Divine force, or nature) and the Many (gods). The One in African thought should be understood in terms of communal oneness. Whatever the debate among the Yoruba religious scholars regarding the term *Irunmale,* it does imply the plenitude, manyness, and the communality of the Divine. Modupe Oduyoye, in her discussion of Yoruba religious etymology, raises the question whether *Irunmale* means four hundred Divinity. She insists, following Idowu, that the word has no reference to number. For her, the term could mean literally four hundred or even 1,440 Divinities. Odudoye takes the term to be an explanation of the immense attributes and majesty of one God.

Though these scholars speaking from within the culture probably know better and need to be taken seriously, one cannot help but be struck with the fact that the Yoruba, as many African peoples, have numerous gods.[35] The question then remains why the insistence on denying plurality. Whether the word *Irunmale* is etiological or not, the concept of the Divine One and Many is still present. Though variously conceptualized, the unique pervasive One diversifies into many—seen as Parent with child(ren), Creator with creatures, Essence and personifications, or Spirit and prolations. The process of Divine becoming in traditional African religion is based on the African emphasis on generativity and is also compatible with the plurality of gods.

The concept of Divine unity and multiplicity among the Dinka of Africa (southern Sudan) has been clearly articulated by Godfrey Leinhardt.[36] Leinhardt shows that the Dinka believe in one supreme force, *Nhialic,* which is all pervasive, but they also maintain the existence of other Divine personifications, gods who are related to one another. In this context, *Nhialic* seems to be the general term referring to the Divine nature shared by the particular gods—Deng, Garang, Macardit and Abuk.[37] The concept of familial communal relationality also comes into play in the Dinka concept of the Divine. For example, one hymn cited by Leinhardt reads:

> Garang Son of Deng has fallen from above.
> If People assemble in the byre it is life
> Kur, and Abuk and Ayi Nyang. . . .[38]

The gods are not separated from one another but are connected by virtue of their common Divinity or nature, which they derive from the all-pervasive force that is their common substance.

Malcolm MacVeigh provides some data for dealing with reference to the Supreme or High God in personalistic-monotheistic terms in African settings. Though he himself speaks of God in monotheistic terms, he provides anthropological data that show Africans referring to gods using the plural terms. MacVeigh's data convey the idea of communality inherent in the African concept of the Divine. For example, he quotes a conversation between Edwin Smith and an elderly African priest in which Smith represents the African priest as saying, "summan [charms] spoil the gods; they take the attention and religious service away from the gods."[39] Whatever the merit of the statement, the concern here is to show that Africans themselves have often referred to multiple gods rather than a singular God who is supposedly the only true God.

That there may be a great God among the gods is unquestionably African, but that this god is the only true God is not African. Also, the idea that worship of these gods is an encroachment on the right of the High God is definitely not African, but imported.[40] If monotheism means the recognition of the existence of a chief among the gods, then the concept is applicable to traditional African no religious contexts. But, on the other hand, if it means the singularity of one single personal God who alone deserves worship, then this concept is alien to traditional African no religion.

That many gods existed in the African tradition from the time of the ancient Egyptians to the present is not debatable; however, the concept of oneness also existed. The question that faces us is the nature of this One. Traditional religious Africans believe in a great power that they see working in the world. Africans also believe in a personalized supreme being identified with such personal names as Chukwu, Leza, Mulungu, Nzambi, Nkulunkulu, and Olodumare. The problem is that their views of how these two concepts are related to each other have not been thoroughly examined.[41] The evidence strongly supports the idea that it is the power or vital principle that is one, and not the gods. The gods are numerous and diverse personifications of that single all-pervasive power. The purpose of the diversification is the continuous actualization of the One through personifications within communality.

MacVeigh notes that in the mind of Africans, conceptions of "the relation between this power and the gods are confused and varied."[42] The confusion arises from the condemnation of the African gods and the ontological separation of the supreme god among these gods from the rest. Hence, Africans, particularly African scholars, have come to confuse this singular power with a singular personal god. This passage from Edwin Smith cited by MacVeigh shows the problem clearly:

> The African view of God is characterized by ambiguity. There are Africans who make no distinction between God and Mana, [Ntu, or Chi]. Others identify god with an impersonal "cosmic Mana" some personify God as cosmic Man and still others distinguish God from Cosmic Man" talking of God as person a specific entity which is worshipped.[43]

A fuller discussion of the term *Mulungu* may help clarify the problem. There are two meanings of *Mulungu* recorded by early anthropologists. One meaning is a personal being regarded as the head of the gods, the chief creator. The second meaning is the impersonal summation of supernatural powers, which is not personified. It is often referred to as that "with no face, hands, legs, or body, does not speak, hear or see everywhere at once, and does whatever it wishes: this impersonal force is sometimes also seen as sheer mind and a very great mind albeit not a rational mind."[44] This does not mean, of course, that this force is purposeless; its sense of purpose is revealed as this force becomes particular gods. Another example of the impersonal/personal problem in the African conception of the Divine comes from the work of the anthropologist Cecil Hopegood. According to Hopegood, it is not quite clear whether the Tonga "always think of Leza [God] as a personal being or as an impersonal force."[45] In fact the Tongas refer to the activities of nature and to the god as father. The gods are in effect embodiments of this power. Without this power the gods will not be God.

SUMMARY

This discussion points to two facts: The concept of *the One* is present in African religions, but so also is the concept of *the Many*. This cannot be called either polytheism or monotheism. Idowu, in defending African traditional religion against the charge of polytheism, states emphatically, "God in African religion is not polytheistic but it is monotheistic."[46] This is only partially correct. The concept of the Divine as community actually does more justice to African conceptions of God. For this we need another term: a word like *communotheism,* a community of gods. Community, in the African sense, will reflect better the affirmation of both the One and the Many than the categories of monotheism and polytheism. The noun *communotheism* communicates the idea that Divinity is communal.

The arguments so far support the idea that African conceptions of the Divine can be said to be communal Mbiti, in his work, *Concepts of God in Africa,* implicitly acknowledges that the concept of a community of gods is present among various African peoples. Mbiti identifies many African peoples who think of God as having a family. For example, the idea of communal Divinity is revealed among "the Ndebeles and Shona Triads, according to which, God exists as *Father Mother and Son.*"[47] The Igbo also have sons and daughters of God that are not human beings. Mbiti also notes that among African peoples such as the Bari and the Tiv of Nigeria, God is said to have brothers and sisters.[48]

Mbiti makes a distinction (I think rightly) between these gods who are sons and daughters of the supreme Spirit and those spiritual beings who are messengers and beings of ontologically inferior and subordinate status.[49] The communality among the gods must be maintained, since in African settings, belonging is the key to existence. This belonging is not mainly voluntary belonging, but it is, as Mbiti has so well stated "I belong therefore I am," the sine qua non of existence.[50] If the so-called Supreme Being has any daughters or sons, the Being can no longer be considered singular, even in authority. To think this way, even the supremacy of this Being is dependent on the relation that this Being has with others.

For some African scholars to say that African religions are monotheistic and, at the same time, to acknowledge several particular entities within this Divinity, is simply to create confusion. We must look for new ways to describe the concept of Divine among African peoples unless monotheism is interpreted to mean one Divine community united in relationality. Even with this interpretation, we need to maintain also that the Divine community is diversified into personalities who are distinct, yet fundamentally related. If the word monotheism does not allow for such redefinition, then we have no choice but to opt for a different word.

If the gods share in the same nature as one family, the supremacy must then be given to their common nature not to one particular supreme personality. When it is seen in this sense, the concept of communality appears to be more appropriate than monotheism in defining such a concept of the Divine. Because they share a common nature, the gods form an inseparable community.

From Idowu's discussion, it is obvious that among the Yoruba, not every spiritual Being is considered a child generated by the so-called Supreme Being. Fundamental relationality and common sharing of nature, which is due to generative interconnection, attains to the African concept of child and parent. This relational principle can be seen in Idowu's discussion of the one arch-Divinity who is seen among some Africans as the Son of God. Idowu, recognizing that this similarity in nature also makes the progeny of a Divine Being, god, states:

> Orisa-nla [arch divinity among the Yoruba] is definitely a derivation partaking of the very nature and metaphysical attributes of Olodumare. Hence he is often known as Deity's son or deputy vested with the authority and power of royal sonship. . . . Olokun [Benin] is known as the Son of Osanobwa vested with power and majesty by his Father. All Akan divinities are called sons of Nyame.[51]

Because those beings who are considered sons or daughters of god are part of the Divine community, statements like Idowu's underscore the concept of generative interconnection in African ontology and cosmology. Such statements also point to an African worldview of the Divine as fundamentally relational and interconnected.

In my personal experience in Igbo traditional religious settings, I never heard a particular god referred to as the creation of the Divine, but as one generated by the Divine, as in birth. This is why the ancestors are never considered gods. The generation of the gods is different from the idea of creation that is applied to humanity and other spirits; they also share in divinity but not as the gods do. The concept of generativity serves to augment the idea that an adequate way to conceive of God in African contexts may be in communal terms.

Temporal functional subordination is also present in the African concept of the Divine. This can be referred to as a hierarchy of responsibility within community. In a telephone conversation with Mazisi Kunene, he insisted that the distribution of responsibility is not hierarchical, but must be seen as historical—something that changes with time and with age. In fact, he went so far as to state emphatically that the human being is not necessarily superior to an insect; rather, there is distribution of responsibility. The key then is mutuality. We live in a mutually interdependent world. In this world, everything possesses some level of intrinsic value.[52] This is necessitated by communality and relationality.

Mazisi Kunene documents how the Africans in Zululand perceive the interaction within the Divine community. Kunene has pointed out that the things in the Zulu epic, *Anthem of the Decade,* are to be interpreted symbolically. For example, while lightning is a manifestation of the god Sodume, the lightning in and of itself should not be called a god. This does not devalue the relation of Mvelinqangi (the king of the gods) to the other gods and goddesses in the epic. The interactions of these beings with one another, their joys and their frustrations, point to a communality undergirded by a sense of fundamental relationality. According to the epic, the Daughter of the King of the gods (sometimes referred to as the Daughter of Heaven) and the other gods share in the creative and recreative process. This relationality is so strong that at the end of the epic the Daughter of Heaven turns to a god and goddess who have been destructive and pronounces:

> She and all of us and Man and all his fellow animals, truly are relatives in the sacred movements of the cosmos. With each cycle we shall grow and be fulfilled.[33]

In the pronouncement of the Daughter of Heaven, the African concept of unalienable belonging is underscored. For the Zulu as with some other African peoples, there is a strong concept that a bond binds the gods within the Divine community.

We may then conclude that the conception of the Divine in Africa is not adequately described by monotheism or polytheism. The African concept of the Divine is communal in nature, better called *communotheism.*

NOTES

1. Edmund Ilogu, *Christianity and Igbo Culture* (New York: NOK Press, 1974), 201.
2. Mbiti, *African Religion and Philosophy,* 104.
3. Ibid., 113.
4. H. Richard Niebuhr, *Radical Monotheism and Western Culture* (New York: Harper and Row, 1970).
5. David Westerlund, *African Religion in African Scholarship: A Preliminary*

Study of the Religious and Political Background (Stockholm: Almquist and Wiskell, 1985). Among the scholars who have maintained the idea of monotheism are J. B. Danquah, John Mbiti, E. Bolaji Idowu, and Emefie Ikenga-Metuh. See also Malcolm MacVeigh *God in Africa: Conceptions of God in African Traditional Religion and Christianity* (Cape Cod, Mass.: C. Stark, 1974), 12.

6. Idowu, *African Traditional Religion.* See particularly chapter 5, "The Structure of African Traditional Religion," 137–202.
7. There is a curious interplay of Chi and Ndu. Chi seems sometimes to refer to one's tutelary god as well as the flow of spiritual energy in and to one's spiritual destiny. Ndu, on the other hand, is life force and one's life cannot be separated from one's Chi. I propose that the Igbos philosophers should speak of ChiNdu = total life force.
8. Idowu, *African Traditional Religion,* 149.
9. Kwesi Dickson, *Theology in Africa* (New York: Orbis Books, 1984) 58–59.
10. Joseph B. Danquah, *The Akan Doctrine of God* (London: Lutterworth Press, 1944), 1.
11. Nomological is a combination of the Greek words *nomos* (name) and *logos,* which is here used to mean the study of names.
12. Danquah, 8.
13. Danquah, 7–8.
14. Danquah, 80.
15. Edwin E. Smith, "A Note On Mulungu," in *African Idea of God,* ed. Edwin Smith. (London: Edinburgh House Press, 1966), 58–60.
16. Ibid. in Smith "A note on Mulungu."
17. Danquah, 28.
18. Ibid., 29.
19. Danquah, 7.
20. See Janheinz Jahn's discussion in which his argument is based on the vitality of the concept embodied within the word Muntu, which is a derivative of Ntu. Janheinz Jahn, *Muntu* (Paris: Editions du Seuil, 1958), 15–16 and 105–32. See also Cullen T. Young "The Idea of God in Malawi" in Edwin Smith, ed. African Idea of God 41; and Placide Temples, *Bantu Philosophy,* trans. Colin King (Paris: Presence Africaine, 1959), 95–111.
21. See the discussion of the classical attributes of God—omnipotence, omnipresence, and omniscience—in Mbiti, *Concepts of God in Africa* (New York: Praeger, 1970), 3–16. All of these attributes seem to refer to a singular personal being and this is precisely what I maintain is misleading in dealing with African traditional religions.
22. Okot p'Bitek, *The Religion of the Central Luo* (Nairobi: East African Literature Bureau, 1971), 41–56.
23. Danquah, 24.
24. Ibid.
25. Ibid.
26. Mbiti, *Concepts of God in Africa,* 114.
27. Idowu, *African Traditional Religion,* 35.
28. Danquah, 39. See also Westerlund, 30.
29. Idowu uses the term mainly in reference to priestcraft and he states that "the main shortcoming of the divinity system is that it lends itself to priestcraft." See *African Traditional Religion,* 173. The same, of course, can be said of

the so-called supreme God. For historically the adherents of monotheism have been much more controlled by priestcraft than the communities with diffusive divinity. It can be shown that the so-called polytheistic religions were usually more tolerant of diversity than those which were emphatic about monotheism.

30. Danquah, 8.
31. Mbiti, *African Religion and Philosophy,* 117.
32. Mbiti, *African Religion and Philosophy,* 107.
33. Geoffrey Parrinde, *West African Traditional Religion: Belief and Practices of the Akan, Ewe, Yoruba, I[g]bo, and Kindred Peoples* (1949; reprint, London: Epworth Press, 1977), 21.
34. Illogu, 35.
35. Modupe Oduyoye, *The Vocabulary of Yoruba Religious Discourse* (Ibadan, Nigeria: Daystar Press, 1971), 17–21. See also E. Bolaji Idowu, *Olodumare: God in Yoruba Belief* (London: Longman, 1975), 68.
36. R. Godfrey Leinhardt, *Divinity and Experience: The Religion of the Dinka People* (Oxford: Clarendon Press, 1960).
37. Leinhardt, 57.
38. Leinhardt, 86.
39. MacVeigh, 23.
40. Ibid., 35.
41. MacVeigh, 16.
42. Ibid., 16.
43. MacVeigh, 120.
44. Smith, "A Note on Mulungu," 58.
45. Ibid.
46. Idowu, *African Traditional Religion,* 135.
47. Mbiti, *Concepts of God in Africa,* 115.
48. Ibid.
49. See Mbiti, *Concepts of God in Africa,* particularly, chapter 11, "God and Other Spiritual Beings."
50. Mbiti, *African Religion and Philosophy,* 107.
51. Idowu, *African Traditional Religion,* 169.
52. Mazisi Kunene, author of *Anthem of the Decade* (1968; reprint, Ibadan, Nigeria: Heinemann, 1981).
53. Kunene, Anthem, 15 verses 23–26.

Three

AFRICAN COMMUNAL DIVINITY: EGYPT AS EXAMPLE

This chapter will focus on the African conception of the Divine as seen in ancient Egypt. The argument of this chapter is that the Divine in ancient African Egypt was seen as a community of gods. This Divine communality is an African concept that influences and is manifest in Tertullian's idea of the Divine as manifested in the Trinity.

My discussion of the African Egyptian concept of the Divine owes much of its form to Eric Hornung's discussion. He presents three strands of opinion concerning the concept of God in ancient Egypt; these are also applicable to Africa in general. In his work, Hornung lists three interpretations of Egyptian conceptions of the Divine: (1) the Egyptians were essentially monotheistic; (2) they were primarily polytheistic; and (3) they held the presence of both oneness and plurality in the Egyptian concept of the Divine.[1]

For many of the scholars that Hornung examines, ancient North African conceptions of God have been an enigma since the early nineteenth century. One of the major issues concerning conceptions of God in North Africa, Egypt, and its adjacent neighbors in Africa has been the relation between monotheism and the plural realities of the Divine. The debate has been carried on since the early eighteenth century.

EGYPTIAN DIVINITY AS MONOTHEISTIC

Hornung documents the attempt of the early nineteenth-century Egyptologists to cleanse Egypt of any taint of "primitive" idolatry and to show that ancient Egyptians expressed a higher religious thought that was described as monotheistic. Monotheism, according to these Egyptologists, meant a singular personal being. They took great pains to show that this monotheism was the true essence of Egyptian conceptions of Deity.[2]

This argument was in agreement with the search for a universal center that overtook western scholarship during the Enlightenment. One of the marks of the Enlightenment was a search for one universal humanity unadulterated by culture, race, religion, or particularities. To do this, Enlightenment scholars armed themselves with the concept that the Divine had to be one, not only in essence but in person. Plurality was considered impure, a degeneration in the understanding of God.

Hornung notes that some French Egyptologists maintained that there had always been a monotheistic interpretation in the Egyptian concepts of God. Many of them, such as Emmanuel de Rouge, argued that the Egyptian religion was originally and fundamentally monotheistic. According to de Rouge, the

> "first characteristic of [Egyptian] religions is the unity [of God] most energetically expressed as God, One Sole and Only; none other with him—He is the only living Being—living in truth."[3]

For de Rouge "one idea predominates, that of single and premier God everywhere and always, it is one substance, self-existent and unapproachable light."[4] By unity, de Rouge means a single personal god, not a unity of communal members. His inability to find a frame in which the presence of the unity of the Divine and the plurality of gods could cohere convinced him that the Egyptian conception of the Divine must be monotheistic. He was convinced that "the Egyptians believed in a self-existent God who was One being who had created man [sic] and who had endowed him [sic] with an immortal soul."[5] This God, for de Rouge and his fellow monotheists, is "without second."[6] Again, from the way Hornung discusses the issue, de Rouge, Le Page Renoufe, and other French Egyptologists (and some German scholars) concentrated mainly on those aspects of Egyptian religious thought that dealt with the Oneness of God. The One for them was more real and truer than what they saw as the later designations seen in various Gods.[7]

This monotheistic position can also be supported by the work of other Egyptologists who have translated Egyptian hymns. For example, the idea that there is a strong conception of the One is represented vividly in this passage from Lucie Lamy:

> Before there was any opposition, any yes and no, positive and negative;
> Before there was presence or absence, life or death, heaven or earth;

> There was but one incomprehensible power, alone, unique, inherent
> in the Nun, the indefinable cosmic sea, the infinite source of the
> universe outside of any notion of Space and Time.[8]

This vision of an original unity of the One, which is an undifferentiated, incomprehensible power hidden from human knowledge, seems to support the concept of an original singular, personal monotheism. This vision has been emphasized by those who believe the monotheistic conception of God is primary, implying that monotheism has superior and purer spiritual significance over polytheism.

One point seems to have been correct in the thought of those who advocated monotheism. The idea of the One was present in the Egyptian conception of the Divine, as it was also found in several other African areas and articulated by various African writers who promote the idea that the Concept of God within African traditional religion is monotheistic.[9] What is false is to assume that this oneness is an entity approximating a personality. It is even more false to assume that this One is a static, immovable entity. The oneness could be described better as that which all the gods share in common—Divinity, Godness, Energy, Substance, Nature and or Power—or some manner of Force whose intensive and extensive presence is a particular mode of being God, distinguished from other modes of being. Misunderstanding results from attributing the fallacious categories of singularistic personality, static monotheism or pure polytheism (gods that are fundamentally separated and unrelated) to the peoples of Africa, both ancient and modern.

We learn also from some Egyptologists that a number of Egyptian sources suggest that the one substance is the primeval waters from which the Primeval One (seed) emerges. This one is not a static Aristotelian Immovable Mover. The One is fluid becoming, a force that pervades the various gods. The fluidity of this pervasive cosmic principle is exemplified in the hymn "Becoming One":

> Hail you, O Atum!
> Hail to you, O Becoming One who came into being of himself!
> You rose up in this your name of High hill,
> You came into being in this your name of "Becoming one."[10]

This One moves around in an undifferentiated state until the process of becoming is initiated or personified as god in a particular historical center.

This One, of course, can become more than one god. In one of the coffin texts* which date during the Old** Kingdom period, (14th century BCE) these words are put into the mouth of the One who rose out of the primeval waters:

> when I was still alone within the waters, in the state of inertness,
> before I found anywhere to stand or sit,
> before Heliopolis had been founded
> that I might be therein.[11]

This idea of a becoming Divine principle that remains in a state of fluidity and continuous extendibility or differentiation leaves no room for a singular personal, absolutely immovable deity. The Divine in this case becomes something that interacts with the universe by becoming differentiated through generative impulses and creative reaching out.

According to R.T. Rundle Clark, the emergence of gods from the vital source is continuous and infinite. This emerging-ness is repeated ritualistically every year, to show that the well-known gods, such as Re, Thoth, and Ammun, have emerged out of the One primeval source.[12] The ritual implies that gods are continuously emerging from the primeval water that is the womb that begets the gods. During the Middle Kingdom, Nun (the primeval waters) is referred to as the "father of the gods," the source from which "the gods indeed originated, in Divine form."[13] If this is the case, the mystery for us is to conceive how this one inscrutable and incomprehensible Power becomes many and how this force becomes personified as god or gods. So, the primeval, undifferentiated one in the Nun can be seen as the nonpersonal ground of which the gods are personifications.[14] The failure to see the diversification of the one into many limits the monotheistic perspective.

Garth Fowden maintains that while politically dominated by foreign powers such as Greece and Rome, Egypt's many gods served a strong gravitational pull on people from different geographic areas. For example, the worship of Egyptian gods was common during the Greco-Roman era.[15] Fowden's comments are notable in this regard: "Of all the wonders past, present, natural and man-made that Egypt had to show, it was her gods and her temples that most caught the imagination of foreign visitors."[16]

* Texts found in Burial Coffins in upper Egypt.
** There are three periods in the historical Construct of Ancient Egypt. Old Kingdom, Middle Kingdom latter Kingdom

Egyptian, religious belief was not easily fused with the religious thought of the conquerors. African Egyptians, while accepting as necessary the political rule of the foreigners, were still able to reject religious colonialism. This is not to argue the absence of syncretism, however, because evidence of syncretism can be found in the history of Egypt. In fact, syncretism, within Egyptian religious thought and in interaction with foreign religious thought, was necessitated by the conception of the Divine as community (a search for relationship that allows the worshipers to deal with differences). Syncretism seems to be a sign that pluralism is at work. Hornung articulates this very clearly:

> It is clear that syncretism does not contain any "monotheistic tendency," but rather forms a strong counter-current to Monotheism—so long as it is kept within bounds. Syncretism softens henotheism, the concentration of worship in a single god, and stops it from turning into Monotheism, for ultimately syncretism means that a single god is not isolated from the others: in Amun one apprehends and worships also Re, or in hermachis other forms of the sun god. In this way the awareness is sharpened that the divine partner of humanity is not one [singular] but many.[17]

The writer of the *Egyptian Hermes* provides examples of African Egyptians' identifying their Divinity within an alien deity that shared similar nature or character in ritual and appellation.[18]

Allan Gardiner gives examples of name swapping among Egyptian gods and other gods as an example of syncretism in Egypt.[19] To share in a name is an acknowledgment of kinship. When the Egyptians swapped names they were acknowledging a synthesis of two gods based on kinship. This fusion does not necessarily mean that the personal god of one village was the same, in reality, as the Divine personification of another village, but the gods were easily identified as having the same nature, having come from one primary source. Africans in Egypt were accustomed to the idea of both commonality and uniqueness of the gods.

Hornung insists that for the Africans in ancient Egypt, the gods were similar, on the one hand, and different on the other. This oneness and manyness, similarity and difference, is more adequately represented by the concept of community. This lends support to the thesis of this discussion that the Divine is a community.[20]

EGYPTIAN DIVINITY AS POLYTHEISTIC

The second strand mentioned by Hornung in his work is the conceptual-ization of the Divine that stresses the importance of the many in ancient African Egyptian religious understanding—the pluralistic, differentiating aspect of the Divine. Adolf Eerman emphasized the idea that polytheism was the predominant idea in Ancient Egypt. Accordingly, one may see the works of Adolf Eerman, James Henry Breasted, and A. Wiedemann as rejecting the claims that Egyptian religion is monotheistic.[21] They maintained that Egyptian religion in ancient Africa was polytheistic. To Breasted, in particular, the early Egyptian religious system was an accident and a chaos of contradictions. He states this quite vividly in the following statement. For Breasted, the beliefs and the gods were so contradictory that,

> Neither did the theologizing priesthood ever reduce this mass of belief into a coherent system; it remained as accident and circumstances brought it together, a chaos of contradiction. Another result of national life was, that as soon as a city gained political supremacy its gods rose with it to the dominant place among the innumerable gods of the land.[22]

For them the multiplicity of gods was not seen as superficial but as real and essential to the very concept of the Divine in Egypt.[23]

EGYPTIAN DIVINITY AS COMMUNAL

The third strand of interpretation of the Egyptian conceptualization of the Divine is that the Divine was conceived of both as one and as many. Erik Hornung, Joseph P. Allen, and Sigfried Morenz favor the interpretation that conceptions of God as both one and many were present in the religious mind of the ancient Egyptians.[24] From these, one can argue that the plurality and differentiation of the Deity is a necessary part of the Egyptian concept of the Divine, as well as the concept of oneness. To quote Hornung again:

> For the believer, every deity is a separate figure with unmistakable features, among which are certain characteristics that are shared with no other deity. *In our study of the Egyptian conception of god these individual qualities of particular gods are less important than those that are shared in common with all the gods and that provide evidence for what, in the Egyptian eye, a god was.*[25]

The emphasis on the communal elements among the gods takes seriously the fundamental relatedness of the gods (in terms of kinship) with one another. This relationship is one reason why I reject polytheism as an adequate description of Egyptian religion. Polytheism seems to emphasize the difference among the gods rather than their commonality.

Another scholar who supports this point is Sigfreid Morenz. Morenz, in *Egyptian Religion*, maintains that in ancient Egypt the Divine was seen as "the potential one that becomes many."[26] Joseph P. Allen is also convinced that the Egyptians maintained this balance of the one and the many as will be shown below.[27] Allen also maintains that fundamental to the Egyptian theology in all periods is the notion of the primordial monad, a single source from which all existence, including the existence of the gods is derived; this is conceptualized in the God Amun in whom the fullness of the nature of the gods dwells.[28] Accordingly, the ancient Egyptians maintained that before the creation of the world, the Divine existed as an externally undifferentiated seed of potentiality, floating in primeval waters, while nonetheless being potentially plural. In fact, the African Egyptian even went so far as to see this as an egg with twins within it. Or it was understood sometimes as a hermaphroditic figure. But this seed is not a god, though it does become a god and engenders many gods. One passage in the *coffin texts* dated in the *Old Kingdom* has the god that emerged out this primeval seed within the waters regretting that it had no progeny. The passage reads:

> O you that arose in your arising, O you that came into being in this your name of Kophri, you are that did say, "Would that I had a son to cleanse me when I appear in my might and bring me acclaim in the pure land."[29]

A description of the primeval one, who moves from being a seed within the primeval waters to One who can impregnate itself and reproduce, confirms the ever-present idea of the One and the Many in the Egyptian concept of the Divine. In one of the passages, are these seemingly contradictory words: "God himself [*sic*] is existence. He endureth without increase or diminution, He multiplieth himself millions of times, He is manifold in forms and in members."[30] In about the tenth century B.C.E, this One was described as a "being whose birth is hidden, whose evolutions are manifold."[31] This primeval One was also referred to as the "Divine form who dwelleth in the form of all the gods."[32] While the constant reference is made to One, this One does not seem to be one particular god for all times. Egyptian history shows that the One was identified with several different gods at different times. This should not be surprising, for it has been noted above that the One is the form of all the gods. Hence, the term monotheism seems to be an inadequate designation.

The plurality that is achieved through the process of generativity or procreation raises the question whether this is not degeneration of the nature of the Divine. Morenz, Allen, and Hornung contend that the Egyptians saw the idea of a plurality of gods as an improvement rather than a degeneration. A single nondynamic, nongenerative being would be an incomplete being. The yearning for a child cited above implies a negative attitude toward being alone and a positive attitude toward generativity. This turns the table on the understanding that God, conceived as an abstract singular principle, is superior to concrete plural personifications.

Morenz maintains that the "Egyptians put into order and systematized the large number of deities which developed historically, and they harmonized this multiplicity of deities with the idea of a single Monad."[33] This monad was described as that which embodies in itself all potentialities—both personal and impersonal—and does not remain one but becomes many. Thus, the reference to this primeval One as the "becoming one," which we find in Egyptian prayers, is fundamental to the ancient Egyptian conception of the Divine. The Divine is a dynamic being that continuously multiplies itself infinitely.

Morenz, perhaps because he is a Christian, tempers this plurality by maintaining that "the ordinary people in ancient Egypt probably visualized god as a single personal figure invested with a full panoply of power and in fact desired that God should be represented this way."[34] Thus, according to Morenz, "in the mind of the [Egyptian] believer the multiplicity of gods or some of them at least becomes fused with the one god whom he/she visualizes, as he/she worships this God as one encompassing reality."[35] However, Morenz is not clear as to whether some Egyptians worshiped more than one god at a time. If one takes Morenz's statement as referring to henotheism, the problem is only partially solved. The idea that the Egyptians had no difficulty ascribing the attributes of the gods of other villages to their own god is not incompatible with the idea of one primeval Divine. If the gods were related and shared the same nature, each god or could have the full panoply of power within the historical circumstance in which such a god is beckoned. This also points to Divine communality since any god can take up the full panoply of Communal power because gods shares in the common Divine nature with all the members than of the Divine Community.

Morenz and Allen are of the opinion that ancient Egyptian theologians were concerned with the intellectual relationship between the single monad and the multiplicity of deities. They attempted to show this relation by developing the theory of the Divine personifications in the Ennead.[36] The Ennead, according to a Hermapolitan tradition of the Old Kingdom, was made up of four pairs of gods and the one primary monad. For this group, Thoth became the first seed that emerged in primeval times. But beside him there were

> the Nun, together with its feminine counterpart Nunet. Three other primeval pairs also existed. . . . There were Kuk and Kuket, that is, Darkness as his consort and Huh and Huhet, the boundless flood and his consort and Ammun and Amunet, the hidden one and his consort.[37]

Interestingly, Thoth, who was considered the first emergent one from whom all the other gods emerged, was not given a consort. If the characteristics of self-creativity through masturbation (which is attributed to the first monad) is also applicable here, then Thoth can be seen as both male and female. Looked at this way, even the One is not a mon—but a community of selves. One prayer in the *Egyptian Book of the Dead* (Fourth Dynasty) refers to the One as having souls—"First among the gods. We adore thy Souls for thou did make us."[38] Though the Egyptians had various gods for various local groups, it seems the relation of these numerous gods to the one primary pervasive force—which is the essential Divine nature of the gods—was never questioned until Iknathon and his sun disc monotheism. The belief in the substantial active force and its differentiation into a multiplicity of gods is the basis of the Egyptian notion of the unity and diversity of the Divine.

The question of the One and Many is not a question of uniformity, even in cases where all the gods share the prefix, Re, as in Re-Ammun, Re-Atum or Re-Horus.[39] For the modern person with the desire to simplify, this may smack of mere modalism. However, modalism does not deal adequately with the idea. The rise of Iknathon forced into the Egyptian religious consciousness an articulation of what the gods shared in common. In other periods, such as the Old Kingdom period, this nature seems to have been represented by the primeval waters; in other times, by the blood that flowed from the phallus of Atum, which formed the various gods. Afterward Iknathon, the sun, or Re with its universal efflorescence came to signify the nature that the gods share in common. This being the case, such naming cannot be seen as a move to uniform perception of the Divine. In a section dealing with the "Names and Combination of Gods," Hornung deals with the issue of the supposed Egyptian uniform understanding of the Divine. In response to a presumed monotheistic uniformity in ancient Egyptian thought, Hornung asks: "Must gods be 'equated' with one another until one finishes with the vague, solar-tinged pantheism?"[40] Hornung's rejoinder is emphatic:

> Such an interchange of attributes, which leads towards uniformity, is un-Egyptian; if anything it is Hellenistic. The Egyptians place the tension and contradictions of the world beside one another and then live with them."[41]

The Divine in this particular African context is not just one absolute person who alone has attributes (such as omnipotence, omniscience) not shared with any other. Neither does oneness mean that only a single God, Divine person or god, deserves to be worshiped as true God. Rather, the above statement implies that in the worship of one of the gods, one apprehends the worship of the others. This idea of oneness protects the personal gods within the Egyptian context from being separated from the rest of the community. The gods were therefore radically related within a community of Divinity.

This view of the Divine as community is also supported by the fact that, while not abandoning the local deities in all their multiplicity, Africans in ancient Egypt still held to a single Divine nature by holding to a single source, the primeval waters. The primeval waters could be seen as the womb from which the gods emerge as well as the active substance, or vital force, of which gods are made. In historical contexts, such as that of the New Kingdom in which the Sun becomes the One, the above concept is also applicable.

Sir Alan Gardiner expresses the opinion that the Egyptian conception of god moved from polytheism to monotheism, an opinion which differs from that of the authors we have considered so far. To support his point Gardiner asserts:

> On the one hand the innate Egyptian conservatism, coupled with a keen local patriotism, militated against the suppression of individual differences; the animal heads remained and the system never ceased to be polytheistic. On the other hand, there was a powerful urge towards

monotheism. Not only was the town god declared to be unique and almighty, but his [similar] identity with the gods of certain other towns was asserted in a number of different ways.[42]

One way in which this similarity was shown was by name swapping. For Gardiner, identity was mainly in names and did not reach beyond that. What one sees in the history of ancient Egypt does not bear this out, however. For example, characteristics are sometimes exchanged without an exchange of names—one god or goddess can be said to have similar powers as another. Usually, an exchange of name implies a similarity in character. The names also carry the power of the individual, so that those who share the same name shared in that power. In fact, it was believed that if one knows another's secret name, that one has the power of the bearer of the name. A religious story from ancient Egypt narrates that the goddess Isis obtained power from the god Re by knowing his name. This shows that knowing another's name or sharing the same name implies a sharing of power or characteristic.[43] I maintain that the identity of the gods is in their nature, because the gods derive from one source and share in Divine nature (notwithstanding their historical situation), which for the Egyptians made them god. The sharing of name underscores this.

The idea that the gods share in the same nature does not mean that they have similar responsibilities. The gods sometimes represent various functions that are carried on by the Divine community in the world. Gardiner also shows how the embodiment of the Egyptian gods changed with changing historical situations, and their functions also changed. This point is exemplified clearly by the place of Osiris in the funerary liturgy. In a hymn to Osiris that had to do with a funerary rite, he is referred to as "Lord of eternity, King of the gods, the governor of the company of the gods." At another point he, is "the well-doing Sekhem [Power] of the Company of the gods"; "the great Chief," "the Prince of the Company of the gods."[44] Osiris, in this hymn, seems to take the place of the One and only God. But, the names applied to Osiris must be seen in context of his function as caretaker of the hereafter in which he functions supreme. This, again, is not incompatible with the possibility that other gods will receive such reverential treatment in their spheres of mythic and historical function.

The place of the gods changed, so it seems, depending on the function at hand. This does not change the fact of their godness. One god may be lifted above the others for praise, depending on what is going on in the life of the person who is praying. The concept of Divine relatedness in ancient Egypt contained within it a distribution of responsibility without diminutive consequence to the ontological status as gods sharing in the Divine nature.[45]

The concept of a Divine Becoming offers useful insights into various ancient African understandings of God. It carries with it the idea that the Force personifies itself through internal generative processes as well as through external creative output in which internal connectedness is continuously maintained.

Separationist conceptions of the gods and their total isolation from one another seem foreign to the Egyptian way of conceiving the Divine. Morenz, Hornung, and Allen maintain that even in cases where there was an acceptance of syncretism of two gods, characteristics that belong to a particular god are never vitiated. Rather, the conception of unity and fundamental interrelatedness seems to enhance the prestige of the particular god in question.[46] Unity and relatedness within a community of Divine Beings and within the universe actually enhance the movement of the gods toward a continual realization of their Divinity.[47] This again supports the concept that in ancient Egypt the gods were seen as a community of related beings who are of similar substance, yet very different in their personation and agency.

At this point, Morenz's warning is very important. Morenz warns against confusing the modern concept of person with the concept of the person as understood in ancient Egypt. He contends that while the Egyptian gods were considered personal and unique, a distinction needs to be drawn between this uniqueness and the modern concept of individuality (separation and isolation from community).[48] To use individualistic criteria in terms of sharp discontinuity is an erroneous way to understand the concept of god in ancient Egypt. Personal characteristics when used in reference to gods/goddess should be seen in terms of their relationality. Characteristics that determine godness do not belong to one particular god; they belong to the community of the many who share the same source or essence.

Grant Allen, was essentially right in insisting that when the concept of god in the ancient world or among so-called primitive peoples is considered, it is better that "the great gods be considered as classes rather than individuals."[49] Among the ancients, in Allen's opinion, the term god refers to a class or community of beings who share something in common. From this definition, it is reasonable to conclude that the Divine as applied to ancient Egyptian religious thought can be seen as a community.

No more prominent evidence exists for the conception of the Divine as community in ancient Africa than the Egyptian Symbolic Projection of the Divine into various triads. Egyptologists also tell us that the Egyptians concept of the Divine is triadic, presented in three different ways. From one perspective the gods are described in terms of the primeval One begetting two, as in the case of the triad of the Old Kingdom—Atum-Shu and Tefnut.[50] From another perspective, the Egyptian triads are described in terms of a couple and a child, as in the case of the Twenty-first Dynasty in which one finds Osiris, Isis, and Horus.[51] The third interpretation of the triad is that in which one god is described in such a way that it embodies within itself three gods.[52] Though the symbol of three was expressed through the kinship relations of father, mother, child, it was not restricted to that familial representation. Three was, for the ancient Egyptian, a way of expressing the many or the plural.

The principle of the One becoming Many, as represented by the number three, is expressed in the following statement in Egyptian literature.

All the Gods are three
Ammun, Re, and Ptah without their seconds
His identity is hidden in Amun
His is RE as Face
His body is Ptah.[53]

In the above passage one finds the three major gods of the three major religious centers in the New Kingdom being placed on a par with one another. Here, also, we see the principle of the interpenetration of gods into one another, and yet each continues to maintain an independent existence.[54]

Morenz maintains that for the Egyptians the number three was a sign of unity in plurality. Morenz points out that both "he" and "they" are used in reference to the triad. The importance of the number lies not in threeness itself but in its symbolic interplay of unity and plurality.[55] The discussion, as seen from the evidence gleaned from some Egyptologists leads to a conclusion that this web of intricate triadic interrelations as a means of accessing the gods could only have been produced by a people for whom community was fundamental.

Apart from terms such as *Neter*, which the Egyptians used to refer to particular gods as well as to gods in general, the Egyptians seem to have developed various ways of symbolizing their "company of gods."[56] In addition to the symbols of three, considered above, there was the phrase *psdt* ("Ennead"), which means a group of nine or a group of three squared. The sign of three in the hieroglyphics, according to Joseph P. Allen, is an indication of plurality, while the Enead could be understood as "plurality of plurals."[57] Hornung calls the Enead "the most important classificatory schema, . . . an intensified form of the plural (three times three)."[58] The Enead then could stand for the symbolic perfection of community.

If the Egyptian saw a kind of kinship relation among the gods, then the Ennead and the triadic symbols could be seen as the primordial communal symbol. As a symbol, the Trinity or the Enead can be a basis for speaking of the unity of infinite plural beings in their Being. This idea of kinship makes the gods one and diverse.[59]

Kinship, of course, is what assures the nature of the gods as gods. In the documents translated by J. P. Allen one sees that even in places where Amun is referred to as the only God, two other gods are added to make three, a plural personification of the one undifferentiated original Amun. In some texts the plurality is described in terms of the gods being various embodiments of the One Divine Principle: "The Ennead is combined in your body, your image is every god joined in your person . . . his are the effective forms of the Ennead. . . ."[60] Allen then concludes that the entire pantheon is nothing more than a sum total of that Original pervasive Power that becomes personified while permeating all that it becomes. The theogonic process (the process of Divine personal emergence) is thus the process in which the one undifferentiated nonpersonal but all-pervasive Divine Power, or Force, becomes many and by the generative process of personification.

Becoming as both theogonic (as necessity within the Divine principle) and cosmogonic (involving the need for creative output), relates to the creation of social-religious centers in ancient Egypt—Heliopolis, Hermer-polis, and Memphis. These centers were recognized as having merit within them. Unlike some of their neighbors, such as Israel where there was a strong movement toward a single religious center, Egypt had many centers without necessarily feeling that they contradicted one another. In all of this discussion, it is safe to say that in ancient Egypt, the Divine was conceived as a community, united but diverse. This is so whether this idea is seen from the perspective of kinship or from another basis. In ancient Africa as exemplified in Egypt, the Divine was seen as community of gods.

SUMMARY

Two basic principles emerge for us in the African Egyptian context as we consider the Divine *communality* and *relationality*. Both of these terms raise issues that are also relevant for the human community. Some of these issues shall be considered in chapter four as we consider the African concept of Divinity in Tertullian's work.

In this chapter the writer found that while the gods were understood by the ancient Egyptians as unique as individuals, what the gods shared in common was emphasized more than what separated them. The concept of the uniqueness and individuality of the gods implies a certain degree of freedom and creativity. But even the power of this creativity and freedom must be seen in light of their communality as gods within the Divine. Simply stated, the Divine in classical Africa was understood as a community.

NOTES

1. Erik Hornung, *The One and the Many: Conceptions of God in Ancient Egypt,* trans. John Baines (Ithaca N.Y.: Cornell University Press, 1971), 18.
2. Ibid., 18.
3. See Emmanuel de Rouge, "Etudie sur le Rituel Funeraire des Ancien Eyptien," *Revue Archeologique,* Paris, (1860), 72, trans. Le Page Renoufe, "Conference de la Religion de Ancient Egyptien," *Anales de Philosophie Chretiene* Paris: 5th, ser 20 1889, 330, cited in Hornung, 22.
4. Hornung, 22.
5. E. A. Wallis Budge, introduction of *The Book of the Dead* (New Hyde Park, N.Y.: University Books, 1960), 106.
6. Ibid.
7. Brugsch, collected a series of passages from Egyptian texts deal mainly with the idea of the One in Egyptian religious thought. Brugsch, *Religion und Mythologie* [Religion and mythology] (Leipzig: 1888), 96–99, cited in Budge, 106–7.
8. Lucie Lamy, *Egyptian Mysteries* (New York: Crossroad, 1981), 8.
9. David Westerlund discusses how African scholars have been arguing the point of African monotheism in recent scholarship. He also states that "Danquah held that the Akan knew only one God; everything else is "superstition." *African Religion in African Scholarship,* 30–33. See also John Mbiti, *Concepts of God in Africa* E. Bolaji Idowu, *Oluodumare* and Idowu, *African Traditional Religion.* E. Ikenga Metuh has also argued that the Igbo conception of the Divine is monotheistic. See his article, "The Supreme God in Igbo Life and Worship," *Journal of Religion in Africa* 1 (May 1973): 20–42.
10. This term is taken from the prayer to Atum cited by R. T. Rundle Clark, *Myth and Symbol in Ancient Egypt* (New York: Grove Press, 1960), 38.

11. A. de Buck, *The Egyptian Coffin Text,* 2 (Chicago: Chicago University Press, 1939), 33 as cited in Clark.
12. Ibid.
13. Hornung, 147–48.
14. James Hillman, *Re-visioning Psychology* (New York: Harper and Row, 1975). Hillman suggests that the term *personifyings* be used because it conveys a sense of dynamic activeness that personification seems to lack.
15. Garth Fowden, *The Egyptian Hermes* (Cambridge: Cambridge University Press, 1986), 13–74. See particularly p. 14.
16. Ibid.
17. Hornung, 98.
18. See Hornung, 98; and Fowden, 18.
19. Alan Gardiner, "The Religious Revolution and After," in *Egypt of the Pharaohs: An Introduction* (Oxford: Clarendon Press, 1961), 214–45.
20. See Fowden, 29; and Hornung, 14.
21. Ibid. Hornung.
22. James Henry Breasted, *A History of Egypt: From the Earliest Times to the Persian Conquest* (New York: Scribner's Sons, 1951), 61.
23. Hornung, 17.
24. Hornung, 24. See also, Joseph P. Allen *Genesis in Egypt: The Philosophy Of Ancient Egyptian Creation Account* (New Haven: Yale University Press, 1988 Morenz *Egyptian Religion*).
25. Hornung, 143. Emphasis added.
26. Sigfreid Morenz, *Egyptian Religion,* trans. Ann E. Keep (London: Methuen and Co., 1973), 58.
27. James P. Allen, *Genesis in Egypt: The Philosophy of Ancient Egyptian Creation Account* (New Haven: Yale University Press, 1988), 24–28.
28. Ibid., 23.
29. Clark, *Myth and Symbol,* 42.
30. Budge, *Book of the Dead,* 107.
31. Ibid., 111.
32. Ibid., 112.
33. Morenz, 138. *Egyptian Religion,*
34. Ibid., 138.
35. Ibid.
36. See Morenz, *Egyptian Religion* 138; and James Allen, *Genesis in Egypt* 30.
37. Beatrice L. Goff, *Symbols of Ancient Egypt in the Late Period* (New York: Mouton Publishers, 1979), 22.
38. From the "Papyrus of *Ani,*" as cited in Budge, *Book of the Dead,* 110.
39. See F. W. Read, *Egyptian Religion and Ethics* (London: Watts and Co., 1925).
40. Hornung, 97.
41. Ibid.
42. Gardiner *Egypt of the Pharaoh's,* 216.
43. J. B. Pritchard, *Ancient Near Eastern Text* (1952), 12–14, cited in Hornung, 88. See also Morenz, 22–23, also cited in Hornung, n. 92, 88.
44. "Hymn to Osiris" in Budge, Book of the Dead, 59–61.
45. Hornung, 97. See also Morenz, 143.
46. Morenz, 140–41.
47. Ibid.
48. Morenz, 142.

49. Grant Allen, *The Evolution of the Idea of God: An Inquiry into the Origins of Religion* (New York: Henry Holt and Co., 1897), 269.
50. See Goff, 21; and Morenz, 142–44.
51. Goff, 142.
52. Morenz, 143.
53. James Allen, 62.
54. Morenz, 143.
55. Ibid.
56. See Budge, 111.
57. James Allen, 8.
58. Hornung, 221.
59. Ibid., 9.
60. James Allen, 51.

Four

AFRICAN COMMUNAL ANALYSIS OF TERTULLIAN'S DIVINITY

The discussion so far has led to the conclusion that the Divine in the African world is communal, which provides a general framework for looking at Tertullian's formulation of the doctrine of the Divine Trinity. Tertullian's concept of the Trinity needs to be understood in its African context. Before proceeding to deal with the doctrine, it is important to examine the historical setting of Tertullian's writings.

In Tertullian, African Christianity found a mind capable of synthesizing monistic and pluralistic aspects of the Divine, both of which found within the African Traditional Systems reveal partial aspects of the Divine.

HISTORICAL AND SOCIOCULTURAL CONDITIONING OF TERTULLIAN'S UNDERSTANDING OF THE DOCTRINE

The influences of Stoic philosophy and Christian revelation on Tertullian have been studied very insightfully by others; therefore, this chapter does not concentrate on the study of Stoic and other Greco-Roman influences. This chapter examines Tertullian's Trinity from direction of conceptions of God in various African traditions and from them draws implications for human community. The African perspective has not been given due consideration in dealing with the thought of Tertullian.

Christopher Stead, for example, postulates two possible origins of Christian trinitarian thought—Jewish and Greek philosophy. The Jewish strand maintained the idea that the archangels, Michael and Gabriel, are similar to God's Word and to the Holy Spirit. Also important for the Jewish origin of trinitarian thought is the separation of wisdom and *logos,* which appears in Judeo-Hellenistic literatures. Stead also suggests that the Stoic rational principle (which suffuses everything in the universe) also had an impact on the development and articulation of the trinitarian doctrines of the church fathers. The plurality of divine persons within the Divine community can also be deduced from the *familiantrias* of God revealed in the *Timeaeus* of Plato. At this point in Plato's work a reference is made to three—God, Wisdom (the consort of God), and *Logos* (their ruler son).

There are African influences on Tertullian's thought. The problem is that these influences on the conceptions of God in the thought of Tertullian have not been considered. In fact, not even the possible influence of the Egyptian concept of Divinity has been considered. This presents some particular concern, considering Egypt's proximity to Tertullian's geographic location. Tertullian lived in Carthage, which was part of what is called Libya today. In his thought, the African penchant for holding the One and the Many in balance through communal connectedness shows forth. The trinitarian theology of Tertullian seems to have been influenced by three traditions in Africa at the time. First, is the African tradition and its systems of metaphysics coming from Egypt and its neighbors. Leonard E. Elliot-Binns,[1] while maintaining that the African natives of Africa, such as the Berbers, had very rudimentary knowledge of God or none at all, mentions nonetheless that Tertullian seems to be a mixture of Phoenicia and African indiginous peoples. In spite of the fact that Elliot-Binns considers that all the foreigners in Africa did intermarry with the indigenous peoples, he refuses to admit the natives made any philosophical or religious impact on foreigners. He is hesitant to accept that Tertullian's philosophical frame of mind has anything to do with indigenous African influence. However, he admits that the North African church architecture has more affinities with Egypt than with Rome.[2] Egypt for him, however, is not Africa proper.

A second influence was the Stoic philosophy that provided Tertullian with certain linguistic-philosophical concepts with which to communicate the African culture of his time to the Christian world. A third influence was the biblical revelation from which Tertullian received the idea of Oneness and the revelation of Jesus as Christ, which opened the possibility for dealing with the Divine plurality from his African perspective.

The complex interaction of these three different worldviews and cultures allows Tertullian to encase an African worldview as it relates to the One and the Many, in terms understandable to others. It is to Tertullian's credit that he was able to synthesize all these. The purpose of this chapter is to examine the concept of the Trinity as developed by Tertullian in *Adversus Praxeas* in the light of the African communal concept of the One and the Many.

The African influence is not recognized by interpreters of Tertullian. For example, Peter C. Hodgson, in *God in History: Shapes of Freedom,* sees the trinitarian theology of Tertullian as an adaptation of the classical Roman understanding of history to a Christian framework.[3] Hodgson maintains "the provenance of history was not the Hebrew Bible, despite the importance for it of historical "acts" of God, but Greek and Roman historiography."[4] Hodgson believes that this Greek influence is the basis of Tertullian's interpretation of history, which provides a frame of reference through which Tertullian reads the Hebrew Scriptures. According to Hodgson, this Greek worldview also forms the basis for understanding Tertullian's formulation of the Trinity. There is no indication in Hodgson's work that he has considered the obvious African influence upon Tertullian's trinitarian thought. It is not even raised as a possibility.

Hodgson is not alone. Historians so far have failed to consider that any virtue was inherent in the indigenous cultural context of Africa. Even though it is well known that some of the most influential church fathers were Africans* there is a lack of acceptance that African worldview may have influenced Tertullian's conception of the Divine. The apparent assumption is that every good that occurred in Africa was the result of Roman or European influences. Exceptions, of course, can be found. For example, Lipsius maintained the African character of Tertullian's trinitarianism, though he links it squarely with "African Montanism."[5] The work of Tertullian restates and replies to the question of the One and the Many, which Africans have been dealing with from ancient times to the present. The concept of the One and the Many affects the way the African worships, the question of wholeness, and the relationship of the person to the community. But the question is essentially the same. Tertullian deals with this issue in the form of questions on the Trinity in his *Adversus Praxeas.*[6]

TERTULLIAN'S CONCEPT OF GOD: THE TRINITY AND THE SCRIPTURE

Historical theological development of the doctrine of the Trinity shows that neither the Hebrew Scriptures or the second testament of Christ speaks explicitly of the Trinity. The Hebrew Scriptures are emphatic in insisting that there is one God beside whom there is no other. There is no stronger indication of the concept of God as a single personal being than in the great Shema: "Hear O Israel the Lord your God is one Lord" (Deut. 6:4,

* An *African fathers* such as, Clement of Alexandria, Cyril, Cyprain of Carthage, lanctanctius, Arnobius, Origen, Athanasius, and of Course Augustine of Hippo.

NIV). From the early patristic period (about 120 C.E.), however, one strand, one strand of Christian thought on the Trinity has been the argument that Hebrew Scriptures did teach the plurality of persons within the Godhead. Israel identified its God with Yahweh, one particular God among other gods, who is not only greater than any other, but later came to be regarded as the only God. Interestingly, Israel did not explicitly deny the existence of other gods; rather, Israel argued that its own God was the most High God, greater than the other gods. Later in the Hebrew Scriptures, particularly in the prophetic literature, we find increasing movement toward the singularity of God in terms of absolute monotheism. In this literature we begin to find such statements as "For I am God and there is non else."*

There are some traces of the "one among the many" in the Wisdom literature. In Proverbs and the Wisdom of Sirach, Yahweh has consorts such as Wisdom or Spirit.

24   When there were no depths I was brought forth, when there were no springs abounding with water.

25   Before the mountain had been shaped before the hills, I was brought forth

26   Before he had made the earth with its fields, or the first of the dust of the world

27   when he established the heavens, I was there, when he drew a circle on the face of the deep,

28   when he made firm the skies above, when he established the fountain of the deep

29   when he assigned to the sea its unity so that the waters might not transgress his command, when he marked out the foundations of the earth.

30   Then I was beside him, like a master workman and I was daily his delight, rejoicing before him always (Prov. 8:24–30; (see also Sir. 24:1–7). NIV)**

We find this same deity sending a messenger, a messiah. In Isaiah, a suffering servant who is almost God, referred to in such phrases as the "mighty God, the everlasting father, the prince of peace, one upon whose shoulder the government shall be" (Isa. 9:6, NIV) is promised to the

* Compare Sirach 24:1–7
** Isaiah 45:22

people. However, these passages in the Hebrew Scriptures fail to do justice to the concept of the Trinity as they are later developed in patristic thought, particularly in Tertullian.

Christians in the first three centuries had various methods of showing that God was a plurality of persons. Reference was often made to passages in Genesis where God is supposed to have beckoned the other members of the Trinity by saying, "Let us make man in Our image" and "Let us go down and confound them" (Gen. 1:26; 11:7). Tertullian used these and other verses with an implicit pluralism in defending his concept of the Divine Trinity against Monarchian attack. In a passage in which Tertullian informs his readers of the prevailing antipluralistic attitudes in relation to the Divine, he also uses the scriptures to show the plurality within the Divine nature. For example Tertullian states:

> If the number of the Trinity also offends you, as if it were not connected in the simple Unity, I ask you how it is possible for a being who is merely and absolutely One and Singular, to speak in plural phrase, saying, "Let us make man in our image and after our likeness" whereas He ought to have said, "Let me make man in my own image and after my own likeness" as being a unique and singular Being?[7]

Tertullian also comments on the statement of God when the human family fell from innocence: "Behold man is become like one of Us" (Gen. 3:22). Tertullian asserts that "[God] is either deceiving or amusing by speaking of plurality, if He is One only and singular."[8] Tertullian, however, recognizes that this interpretation is not consistent with the interpretation given these scriptural passages by the Jewish people to whom the Hebrew Scriptures belongs. Tertullian asks: Who was with God when it was said "let Us"? To which he replies:

> Was it to the angels that he spoke, as the Jews interpret the passage. . . .? or was it because He was at once the father, the son and the Holy spirit, that He spoke to himself in plural terms making himself plural on that very account? Nay, it was because He had already his son close at his side as a second Person His own Word, and third Person also, the Spirit that He purposely adopted the plural phrase, "Let us make" and "in our image" and "become as one of us."[9]

For Tertullian all these scriptural passages point to and speak of the unity of the Trinity,[10] underscoring for him the community of persons within the Divine One.

Another Hebrew Bible passage used by Tertullian in support of his concept of the Divine plurality is the Wisdom passage of Prov. 8:22–25. This passage is for Tertullian an indication of the intrinsic mutual relation of persons within the Godhead. It focuses the plurality within the Divine unity. According to Tertullian,

> the power and disposition (*dispositio*) of the Divine Intelligence is set forth in the scriptures under the name of [Sophia] Wisdom; for what can be better entitled to the name Wisdom than the Reason or the Word of God?[11]

The very speech serves to designate Wisdom as another in the Divine community. To make sure that this is understood, Tertullian states furthermore:

> Listen therefore to Wisdom herself constituted in the character of a Second Person: "At the first the Lord created me as the beginning of His ways with a view to his own works, before he made the earth, before the mountains were settled; moreover before all hills did he beget me" . . . Then again observe this distinction between them implied in the companionship of Wisdom with the Lord.[12]

The trinitarian thought that was developed in the African church by Tertullian can be seen as the basis on which the Christian church in the West built the trinitarian doctrine. This doctrine could not be found in Judaism since the strict monotheism of the Jews prevented them from making any statement that might imply that God is not One. The fear of polytheism precluded the possibility of plurality within the Godhead. For them the Godhead is one in essence; hence, we may need to look for the origin of that which gave this doctrine its form in Tertullian's thought (and in other African forebears) in more than the Hebraic understanding of God.

The emergence of Christianity and the belief that developed concerning Jesus Christ as the Son of God helped the church to formulate the Trinity. Jesus Christ was seen as the Savior of the world. Through a process of theological abstraction from the biblical revelation, Jesus came to be regarded as being of the same nature with the *one Divine principle*. Statements of Paul, such as the "express image of the visible God," (Col. 1:15–21) were used by Tertullian to support his conviction that the Divine is more than one singular individual personal being. This one Divine Force is somehow related to Christ, at a level that is beyond the relation of the Divine to the created order, of which humanity is part. For Tertullian the African, this was an answer to the age-old question of the One and the Many. The issue idea of the relation between God and Jesus Christ is apparently what led Tertullian back to the African question of plurality within Divinity. This raised the problem of his faithfulness to the monotheistic conception of God in the mind of his readers. Many in the church seem to have taken a road that led them to posit a Christ of different substance. The particular group with whom Tertullian debated in Adversus Praxeas posits a singular personal being without differentiable relationships. Seemingly, something more than the scripture influenced Tertullian's interpretation of the Trinity.

In the Christian Testament, particularly in the synoptic Gospels, we find the writers emphasizing the concept of one single God who is the universal creator. However, with this comes an explicit connection with the person of Jesus Christ who is believed to be the Messiah. He is then equated by other writers of the Christian Testament with Wisdom of the Hebrew Testament and the instrumental Word with which God created the world. Thus, we have the Johannine phrase "The word was with God and the word was God" (John 1:1, NIV), and Paul wrote of the wisdom of God (1 Cor. 1:18–25, NIV).

Biblical scholars have argued that, at most, the Gospel writers may have been binary, not trinitarian. They also concede that there is an emphasis on the Holy Spirit in the book of Acts that cannot be easily dismissed. Also, the church came into a world where the Africans of Egypt had emphasized the triadic concept of God for many centuries. Tertullian tapped into the religious sentiment of African worldview as represented by Egyptian concepts; he did this by proposing a trinitarian frame for dealing with the concept of the Divine. Through this use of African categories, Tertullian has left us with a legacy of doctrines that was first revealed implicitly in the scriptures and later made explicit by the church leaders and theologians of the first three centuries. Most of these leaders were African such as Origen, Augustine, and Athansius. Through the use of African cultural-religious sentiment, Tertullian interpreted these implicit scriptural motifs.

Tertullian used the Christian Scripture to nuance his doctrine of the Divine One and Many, but his comment on the temptation passage is most interesting. Dealing exegetically with Matt. 4:3, Tertullian begins with the statement attributed to the tempter. He uses this to show that it was not the whole Divine community that was being tempted but one person from within the Godhead, the Son; he does recognize that the other members of the Godhead had some stake in the outcome of the temptation. The fact that the temptation story quoted below refers both to the Son and the Father confirms for him that Divine is not one single personal being. Commenting on the temptation, Tertullian says,

> here the old serpent has fallen out with himself, since when he tempted Christ after John's baptism he approached him as the Son of God; surely intimating that God had a Son, even on the testimony of the very scriptures, out of which he was at the moment forgetting his temptation: "If thou be the Son of God, command that these stones be made bread," Again "if thou be the son of God cast thyself down from hence; for as it is written He shall give His angels charge concerning thee"—referring no doubt to the Father—"and in their hands they shall bear thee up, that thou hurt not thy foot against a stone."[13]

This drama recorded in the Christian Testament is for Tertullian an assurance that the Divine is indeed a multiplicity of persons.

Tertullian also claimed that the doctrine of the Trinity that he espoused came from "the rule of faith which has come down to us from the beginning of the gospel even before any older heretics much more before Praxeas a pretender of yesterday."[14] Tertullian tells us that his doctrine is from the Gospels. The fact is that while the belief is implicit in the Gospels, the internal relationship among the members of the Divine community is far from being explained within the corpus of the New Testament message. The doctrine in the final analysis is theological extrapolation informed by a specific relational worldview. This worldview is, as I will show, discoverable in the African conception of community.

TERTULLIAN'S TRINITY: A THEORY OF THE DIVINE COMMUNITY

Tertullian marked the move from a mainly cosmological trinitarian language to ontological considerations of the inner relation of the life of God as a community by looking specifically at the other two members of the Trinity. "It is as an African enlivened by the sun, thirsty for water, and nourished by the fruits of his soil that Tertullian pictures the trinitarian procession in the context of creation and sanctification."[15]

For Tertullian, the notion of the Trinity is ideologically connected to the fact of salvation as embodied in the church community. The Trinity is the witness of faith. Tertullian contends,

> the witness of the faith and the guarantee of salvation have as security the three persons. We add mention of the church because where the Three are, the Father, the Son and the Holy Spirit, there is also found the church which is the body of the Three.[16]

The salvation offered to the world, according to Tertullian, is incomprehensible in his worldview without the Divine pluralistic communal framework. The work, the persons, and the revelation of the Divine community through incarnation finds its raison d'etre in symbolic, communal, mutual relationships of the gods (persons) within the Divine, both in terms of ontology and function. For Tertullian, the symbol of the Trinity is the economic and on temporal-functional Trinity which is, at the same time, ontological and immanent through the oneness of sharing one substance. Communality is the foundation of Tertullian's understanding of salvation, for according to this perspective, we are saved by all the members of the Divine community as evidenced in the Trinity consisting in the unitive, participative, reciprocal relationship founded on their common unity.[17]

In describing his Trinity, Tertullian used variegated manners of speech that are important for our present consideration. In describing the Trinity, Tertullian used natural images—metaphors and terms that are taken from the realm of physical nature; and images from sociocultural and political settings. Tertullian did not seem to be bound by the conventional usages of linguistic-metaphorical terms. He used terms that were familiar to his society, while imbuing them with new meanings, which helped to convey the ideas he wished to express. Tertullian's thought was a clear example of semiotic invention. His was an invention made possible by conceiving the Trinity in terms of African ontology and cosmology.

Tertullian used various concepts that are African to describe relation-in-community both in its ontological-equalitarian and functional-temporal-subordinate relations. These included social and political metaphors that must be deciphered for the particular meaning that Tertullian gave to them. One of the social concepts that he used was that of a family. Looking at the family from an African perspective may shed some light on the arguments one finds in Tertullian. Understanding the uses of various terms in Tertullian's work and analyzing them in terms of African worldview will help to illuminate his understanding of the inner ontological as well as the historical objective relationship of the Divine community.

However, before proceeding, it is needful for the sake of clarity, to note that the problem of the Trinity that Tertullian deals with in *Adversus Praxean* is an attempt to provide solution to the problem of the One and the Many. This has always been a concern for African conceptions of the Divine as one and of the personal gods-many who share in the Divine nature. Tertullian insisted that the Divine be considered as a "distribution of the unity into Trinity."[18] Tertullian also claimed that he and those of his party, "since [having been] better instructed by the Paraclete, who is the leader into all truth, believe that there is one God [Divine principle] indeed, but yet under, the dispensation we call the oikonomia."[19] Tertullian claims that this concept as he expressed it, which was the traditional doctrine of the church is exaggerated. We know for a fact that people like Praxeas and Valentinians, along with Homogenes, the separationists and ontological subordinationists, were part of the church when he was writing. Many Christians in the Second Century had different traditions from Tertullian. Moreover, the line had not yet been clearly drawn between orthodoxy and heresy at this time.

Tertullian's doctrine of the Trinity, which I call *the Divine community,* derives from the fact that a second person within Divinity is considered not only Divine, but also a deity in the full sense of the word, though not absolutely identical with the other deities within that community. This raises for Tertullian's trinitarian concept a serious question: Is the second considered something or someone that the Divine community cannot be without—one without whom the Divine community is incomplete and poorer? This someone, this second or third or other, is seen as an intrinsic part of the definition of the Divine communion. Yet, this same one is spoken of as begotten Son. By placing this principle in the center of the Divine communal self-definition, Tertullian essentially makes equality of nature a criterion if not a necessity. Unless this being was in the Divine milieu, and shared in the Divine nature with the other members of the Divine communion, the Godhead is incomplete. The second or the others within the Divine community are necessary members in terms of the trinitarian definition of the Divine. The second member did not become the Son out of compulsion or necessity, and the first is not Father by necessity. Rather they both become so in the initiation of history and by a choice to incarnate in specific roles. The immanent Divine community becomes the functional-temporal community. The plurality is immanent both within the Divine, as it is in itself, and in the midst of the unfolding in historical functions.

Benjamin B. Warfield in *Studies in Tertullian and Augustine* has noted, and rightly so, that the Greek Logos Christology to which Tertullian may have been heir through the apologists, out of "necessity [of] its fundamental postulate," placed the other member of the Divine community as "something less than God overall."[20] The extent to which Tertullian buys into this appears to place some limitation upon the full development of the concept of equality inherent in his idea of immanent Divine plurality of person. But this idea of equality is there, nonetheless, and needs to be untangled in order that one might see clearly how, in Tertullian's thought, the one Divine principle not only diversifies itself into the Many (which are capable inherently of undertaking various functions without thereby diminishing their essential divinity), but the One is inherently plural.

Warfield also maintains that the Greek notion of Logos fails to hold Tertullian's concept of the Divine community. In his own words, "[Tertullian] stretches the logos doctrine beyond its tethers and was already passing in his construction to something better."[21] One sees in Tertullian a man who struggles to maintain a holistic emphasis of the nature of the Divine by holding to a Divine communal image.

DIVINE COMMUNAL IMAGERY FROM NATURAL ENVIRONMENT

Tertullian gives us three groups of images in reference to the Trinity that strongly suggest communality both in its inner order and in its sanctifying effusion: roots-branch-fruit, source-river-rivulet, sun-ray-tip. Tertullian was the first to elaborate such a systematic, though inevitably deficient, cosmological representation of the Divine community.[22] The cosmological representation of the Trinity we find in Tertullian must be placed side by side with other metaphoric representations in order to balance out the ontological and functional representation of the Trinity. For example, the idea that the Divine was not alone, though One, the idea that the Word of God is God and the idea that the Word becomes Son, need to be placed side by side.

Bertrand DeMagarie argues that Tertullian's concept of the Trinity is guided by cosmological reality rather than by intersubjective communication.[23] This does not seem to support the principle that Tertullian lays down. After considering the place of reason and word in the Godhead before creation, Tertullian stated:

> I may therefore without rashness first lay this down (as a fixed principle) that even in the beginning before the creation of the universe God was not alone, since he had within himself both Reason and inherent in Reason, His Word, which He made second to himself by agitating it within himself.[24]

The cosmological illustrations in Tertullian appear to be explanations of the inner ontic relation within the Divine community, which point to intersubjective communication among the members of the Divine community. This is an immanent distinction that makes possible the cosmological emanations. The intersubjectivity is articulated in the relation that Tertullian perceives between the Word and other members of the Divine community:

> The Word therefore, is both always in the Father, as he says, "I and the Father are one" and is always with God, according to what is written, "And the Word was with God; and never separate from the Father or other than the Father, since" "I and the father are one." This will be the prolation taught by the truth, the guardian of Unity wherein we declare that the Son is a prolation from the Father, without being separated from Him. For God sent forth the Word as the spring the river, and sun the ray, for these are (probole) or emanations, of the substance from which they proceed.[25]

The emanations of Tertullian are different from modalism or from Valentinian abstractions. Tertullian's emanations are conceived as actual personifications not just modes or manifestations of one single person. Each personification is an active entity within the Divine community. They relate as actual persons within the history of creation, not as attributes of one particular God-person.[26] The personification of the entities within the Godhead, in Tertullian's thought, is supported by the evolution of the second person. The second person moves dynamically from Reason to Word to Sonship within the Godhead. This movement is made possible by the fact that the second shares in the spiritual substance of the Divine.

To show the unity of substance that supports the ontological connection among the members of the Godhead, Tertullian argues that though they are parts of the tree, they can be considered second in terms of degree. For, the "tree is not severed from the root, nor the river from the fountain, nor the ray from the sun; nor indeed, is the Word separated from God."[27]

Later in the same passage Tertullian reemphasizes this connection by a string of analogies:

> For the root and the tree are distinctly two things but correlatively joined. The fountain and the river are also two forms but indivisible; so likewise the sun and the ray are two forms but coherent ones. Everything which proceeds from something else must needs be second to that from which it proceeds without on that account being separate.[28]

Looking at it from a slightly different dimension, Tertullian's interest does seem to lie in the fact that each part of the tree is fully in the other while still being a distinct part. The root contains the leaves and the branches. The leaves have the branches and the root and every part of the tree within it. The branch contains the rest of the tree within it. Yet, in a real way they are distinct as leaves, branch, and root within the tree. The imagery suggests more phenomenal intersubjectivity than is suggested by a casual look. The Godhead dwells in full in each personifying entity. This way of putting it allows for the integrity of the specificity that is characteristic of each personal member.

The analogies from nature also point to Tertullian's aversion to separationism and underscores his belief in the principle of ontological connectedness. This aversion may explain why Tertullian rejects Valentinian emanations. He states his position vis-à-vis Valentinus as follows: "If any man shall think that I am introducing some probole—that is to say, some prolation of one thing out of another as Valentinian does . . ." such a one in Tertullian's opinion is mistaken.[29] But Tertullian does derive something, actually, someone from another. His disagreement with Valentinus points to a more fundamental difference. For Tertullian this prolation is not that of one thing of a completely different nature, or even of inferior nature from another, but the emergence of something of equal nature from one ground that warrants it to share the same nature.

If the above explanation is relatively accurate, how should one explain the fact that Tertullian is definitely subordinationist in his consideration of the Divine community? The response to this question can be attained by considering the difference between manifestation of the Trinity in history or the economy of human salvation and the consideration of the Trinity before the emergence of history. The difference lies in the distinction that can be made between ontology and historical temporal function. The equality of the three for Tertullian is the result of the fact that they possess the same identical substance and nature, and they share in power of the One whose personifications or prolations they are. The concept of functional subordination is an inherent part of community, and it is not contradictory to equality of nature.

COMMUNAL METAPHORS IN TERTULLIAN'S THEORY OF DIVINITY

In Tertullian's work on the Trinity he uses such words as *Monarchia, Dispositio,* and *Oikonomia,* which convey a sense of communality. These are metaphors that relate to the social sphere.

Tertullian criticizes what he sees as a naive acceptance of the word monarchy and the insistence that monarchy means singleness of rule. The common argument seems to run thus: The Christians had been called from plurality (the assumption that there are different kinds of Divine natures) of gods to worship the only true God. This God is a unity of monarchy and indivisible into any manner of plurality. To this Tertullian replies: "although there is one only God, this God must yet be believed in this Gods economy."[30] The ones against whom Tertullian writes, assumed that the numerical order and the distribution of the Trinity, which was proposed by Tertullian, is a "division of Unity." But Tertullian maintains that he himself does not see "the Unity which derives the Trinity out of its own self as being destructive of unity, rather it is actually supported by it."[31]

Monarchia. Due to the use of the term *Monarchia* as implying absolute, singular, personal rulership by a certain group or individual, any attempt at Divine purification was condemned as polytheistic. Tertullian was accused of preaching two or three gods with different natures because he insisted on the plurality of members within the Divine, even in its unity. Tertullian protested this accusation by stating:

> They are constantly throwing against us that we are preachers of two gods and three gods, while they take to themselves pre-eminently the credit of being worshippers of the One God just as if the Unity itself with irrational deduction did not produce heresy, and the Trinity rationally considered constitute the truth.[32]

Tertullian may have placed himself in this dilemma by an overemphasis on a singular God in his earlier writings—*Apology* and *De Idolatria, Ad*

Marcionem I—which seemed to the people to mean absolute, single, personal rule.

Tertullian perceived the accusation of polytheism as coming from an overly literal understanding or misunderstanding of the term *Monarchia*. As far as Tertullian was concerned the term *Monarchia*, which was commonly used by those who saw well in personal singularistic terms, did not have univocal meaning. It did have reference to the "sole Divine governance" or "one single rulership of the Divine," but in Tertullian's concept this did not mean one single personal rule.

> We say, the sound goes, so even the Latins (and ignorant ones too) pronounce the word in such a way that you would suppose their understanding of the (monarchia) was as complete as their pronunciation of the term. Well then, Latins take pains to pronounce the (monarchia) while the Greeks refuse to understand the (oikonomia) of the Three in one. As for myself, however, if I have gleaned any knowledge of either language. I am not sure that (monarchia) has another meaning than a single and individual rule but for all that this, monarchy does not, because it is the government of one, preclude him whose government it is, either from having a son or from having made himself actually a son to himself, or from ministering his own monarchy by whatever agents he will.[33]

For Tertullian, *Monarchia* does not mean singular personal monotheism. Rather *Monarchia* stands for a fundamental relational base on which a kingdom is founded. The kingdom is never really ruled by one single individual but by a community of persons. The concept of generativity and becoming as a blessing and sign of Divine plenitude, rather than a sign of depletion and entropization, is also implied.

Tertullian seems to think that there is in the Divine, one Community and one Power from which all the members of the community draw by virtue of the one Nature in which they share. Tertullian's view of communal relation affects his understanding of rulership. He does not accept the possibility that one individual can actually carry upon himself or herself the power of the community. Neither can the authority to carry out all the functions within community be bestowed on one person. This idea of communality is revealed in the Tertullian's statement: "No dominion so belongs to one only, as his own, or is in such a sense singular, or is in such a sense a monarchy, as not also to be administered through other persons most closely connected with it and whom it has also provided as officials to itself."[34] It is not merely the fact that several people are involved in the rulership that suggests communality. These persons must be connected fundamentally. Tertullian rejects an atomistic separation of the members of the Divine community and maintains the connectedness on this basis. Tertullian argues that the monarchy belongs equally to all the members of the family, including children. This does not constitute a division of the monarchy. The members of the Divine community in Tertullian's opinion cannot really be separated from it; belonging is forever.

Tertullian's insistence on the indivisibility of the Divine rulership, in spite of the plurality of authority is consistent with his insistence that the members of the Divine community are distinct but not separate. To reinforce this Tertullian continues:

> If, moreover, there be a son belonging to him whose monarchy it is, it does not forth with become divided and cease to be a monarchy, if the son be also taken to be a sharer in it; but it is as to its origin equally his, by whom it is communicated to the son; and being his it is quite as much a monarchy or sole empire since it is held together by two who are so inseparable.[35]

The inseparable nature of the relationship is due to the fact that they share similar substance. Tertullian's argument is this: If those who are not members of the monarchial family can share in the power without destroying the monarchy, how much more can it be assumed that the plurality of persons within the family of similar substance can cause division of power and unity of the monarchy. Tertullian insists, if God can use angels without destroying the Divine community,

> how comes it to pass that [the Divine] God should be thought to suffer division and severance in the Son and the Holy Ghost who have the second and the third places assigned to them and who are closely joined with the father in his [the Divine] Substance?[36]

The other two persons are thus seen by Tertullian as natural members of the substance that indwells the Father. They are in Tertullian's perspective "instruments of God's might and they are the power and entire system of the monarchy."[37] Working from the actual meaning of monarchy in terms of how it functions in reality, Tertullian concludes that while there is one power because the monarchy is one kingdom or community of fundamentally related persons,[38] this kind of rulership does not preclude plurality of rulers or of authoritative functions, especially if the people carrying out the functions share similar substance and, hence, power with the members within the community of rulers.

Tertullian creates a problem by stating in *Ad Homogenes* that God has not always been Father until the economic manifestation of the second person for the purpose of creation. He argues, nonetheless, that the second person was God before becoming Son. The problem is exactly this: How does one explain the apparent notion that God, who is considered eternal in all aspects, is not an eternal Father? One can reasonably conclude that in the thought of Tertullian, fatherhood or sonship categories appear to be in the Godhead functionally and temporally.

For Tertullian, the Divine is not a static and passionless principle. Unlike other church fathers and philosophers of his time for whom the passions were evil, Tertullian did not see the passions as evil in themselves. The Divine or the gods are not impassable. Movement happens within the Divine milieu. It is this movement that explains the fact that there is more than one person within the Divine community. As Tertullian suggested in the following passage:

> For before all things God was alone-being in himself and for himself
> universe, and space and all things, moreover, he was alone, since he
> had within himself both reason and inherent in Reason, the Word,
> which agitate within the Divine [communal] self.[39]

The reason to which Tertullian here refers is equated with ratio (Reason) and Sermo (Seed). For him, this ratio is not a mere abstract attribute but a second person within the Divine who becomes Son as the Word and is begotten for a particular function—of carrying into effect that which was considered and discussed within the council of the Divine community. This purpose includes such matters as the creation of the world, the redemption of the world, and divinization of history through the presence and availability to all creation of that all-pervasive Spirit, which is the essence and definition of Divinity. For Tertullian it is "the very Word Himself who is spoken of under the very name of wisdom and of reason and of the entire Divine Soul and Spirit. He became also the Son of God and was begotten when he proceeded forth from the Godhead."[40]

Tertullian almost falls into the trap of the monotheist whom he is trying to discredit by personifying the substance and claiming that the Father is the full representation of the substance and the two are merely derivatives. But since he has already made clear that he does not mean either ontological subordination or separation, this apparent self-contradiction is avoided. The effect of his internal ontological perception of the plurality within the Divine community is not diminished. The argument that the Father has within him the fullness of the substance will be problematic if the meaning of being god is not also applicable to other members of the Divine community. In Tertullian's thinking, all the members of the Divine community emerge from the same substance—Godhood—though speaking historically the Father is prior, the Son second, and the Holy Spirit third. Regarding the nature of the other members of the Divine community, Tertullian contends that by virtue of allowing the other to emerge from the same substance in a generative sense, "He [the Father] does make Him equal to Him."[41] Within a worldview, such as the African worldview, which does not regard a parent as ontologically superior to the child though the parent is fully grown, the place of each member in the process of emergence becomes less problematic than it appears at first.

Dispositio. The term *Dispositio* used by Tertullian can also serve to nuance the concept of the Divine as community. It can be taken as reference to the internal personal relation between the various dimensions of a person—the body, soul, and spirit—which are in continuous interactions with one another. These interactions are intimate and often nondecipherable. Tertullian's use of the term *Dispositio* can be translated as either "dispensation" or "disposition."[42] The term refers to "mutuality of relations within the Godhead" that cannot be carried out unless, of course, the Divine, prior to historical generative prolation, was a community.[43] The term *Dispositio* is closer to the African concept of intergenerative interconnection based on a never ceasing belonging within the community that fosters a continual and unbroken communication.

Tertullian uses the personal term *allium* in opposition to the neuter *aliud* in connection with dispensation, recognizing that each member of the Divine community as distinct, relational subject/object.[44] From this it may be argued, and rightly so, that intersubjectivity is the ground of Tertullian's conception of the inner trinitarian community of the Divine.

Oikonomia. Another communal metaphor that Tertullian uses is *economy.* For this term he retains the Greek term for household *Oikonomia.* In this case, then, the Trinity is seen as the household of the Divine. The use of the term *economy* implies that they are equally involved in the salvific process. For Tertullian, *economy* signifies the enumeration of the

Divine persons (or the particular members of the community as god) in its scriptural augmentation; it is the manifestation of the Divine "procession" in history by the ordered plurality of lordly and salvific activity.

This economic distinction is not merely external but derives from the internal distinction that is already present in the Divine. In this sense, Tertullian's use of the term *economy* should be distinguished from the use of the term *Dispositio*. But it is the *Dispositio* of the Divine, its "becomingness," which makes the functional distinction in the *economy* possible.[45] The latter refers to inner immanent mutual relation within the community, while the former refers mainly to the outward working of the Divine community as the members are functionally related to one another within creation.

There are three stages in every epoch of the Divine communal movement that one finds in Tertullian. The first is that of the Divine prior to Creation. In the beginning the Divine was alone. The Divine vitality was one nontranscendentally differentiated. This oneness means that there was total equality within the Divine community. Nothing less than god was external to Divine persons. The Divine entities who were within the Divine community and who occupied both Godhead and the entire universe, and space and all things. From this first stage, the principle drawn is this: The Divine was alone as community, particularly since the Divine seems to have been restless (agitated) in this stage.[46]

Within the first stage Tertullian introduced a dialectic, "yet God was not alone." Because the Divine was a community of persons and in that oneness was a plurality of personal entities seeking actualization and self-realization through various historical functions, the Divine cannot be said to be alone in terms of singularity. There were personifications within the Godhead: "God possessed within himself Reason, consciousness and the unspoken Word (thought), Wisdom."[47] For Tertullian these are not voids or abstractions but real personifying entities. The principle is this: since that which is within the Divine cannot be a mere abstraction but must in reality be considered as other persons, Wisdom and Reason must therefore be considered persons.[48] The principle that Tertullian himself sets forth is this: "before the creation of the world, God was not alone since he had within himself both reason and inherent in reason the Word which he made second to Himself by agitating it within Himself."[49] God then was a community before creation. This was a community with no knowledge of another nature until the creation.

In the second stage the Divine generates and creates. It is in this stage that functional procession begins. Gods or persons emerge (not as the existence of a different kind of nature that is not a God-nature) for the purpose of specific functions. The gods are no longer alone as community in time and space. The Divine personifications within the Godhead (existing as "Gods" within God) now take on an external personifying. They are objectified as Word, referred to as Wisdom and, in that process, become second (in the sense of coming after in function) person for the purpose of creation and thus become Son in the functional realm. To show that the same one who was the Reason within the Godhead is the one who became the Word and the Wisdom, ordering and creating the world. Tertullian says "as soon as it pleased the Godhead (Divine community) to put forth into their respective substance and forms of things (different from the pure God substance) the Word was put forth."[50] The principle here is this: The fundamental communal Divinity is also manifested as community in the distribution of responsibility in the creation of the universe.

In stage three, the members of the Divine community reintegrate their experiences in the Divine milieu. The members of the Divine community in Tertullian's scheme return to the substantial level of equality of existence at the end of their temporal functions within history. But this returning into that level cannot be the same as it was when they reached out economically into the world. For at this moment, the members bring with them the actual experience of creation, its fragmentation and their experiences of recreating wholeness. They bring with them experiences of their interaction with the world to enrich the Divine substance as they prepare for a new interaction in a new age. Tertullian takes his point of departure from Paul's statement in 1 Cor. 15:24–25: "When he shall have delivered up the kingdom to God even the Father. . . ."[51] Here Tertullian speaks in terms of the other members' giving up, not their identity, but the result of their functions within history into one pool of Divine experience. One finds, then, in Tertullian, a movement from undifferentiated (in terms of responsibility) communality to connected individuation in which the distributive, temporal responsibility is undertaken, and back to communality in which the fundamental nature is again recognized and reaffirmed and preparation is made to undertake other temporal responsibilities in new epochs. The next phase then, is informed by the total *experiences* of the Divine community. In all these processes, a particular Divine person remains connected and related to the Divine milieu. The

Trinity for Tertullian was not merely a definition of three actual entities within the Divine community, but also a symbol of the historical process of being, belonging, and becoming.

Tertullian being the first in the West to use the term *Trinity,* indicated clearly enough that the "Trinity of one divinity" was not just an economic, but also an immanent Trinity. He was the first to stress the term *person* and to understand it in the metaphysical sense of a concrete individual, a self, which is not separated from its communal connection. He affirmed that the three persons of the Godhead are "one substance"; by "Divine substance" Tertullian meant a rarefied form of spiritual matter.[52] This principle seems to be similar to the African idea of force or power—that substantial element that pervades the universe and becomes personified in various ways.

The idea of common Divine substance helps Tertullian to avoid an ontological subordination. The idea that Tertullian is a complete subordinationist results from his confusing illustrations with reality and from the failure to see community as the basic concept informing his idea of Divinity. For example, it is assumed by some that Tertullian's illustrations[53] are arguments for an ontological subordination in the Trinity. On the contrary, the illustrations demonstrate the common substance and the distinctive form that it takes at various particular points of its dynamic movement. In Tertullian's thought, the Trinity signifies more than any simple triad. The Trinity designates the number three as a sign of infinite Divine plenitude.

For Tertullian, the internal activity must be distinguished from external activity, whether this be creative or destructive. Most external acts that result from ontology do not define the nature of being. In this sense, Tertullian is different from Augustine or Basil. The former based the unity on the concept of love, the Holy Spirit being the utmost expression of that love. The latter saw the unity in the Divine properties that are at the base of, and interconnect with, the hypostasis. Both based equality and unity on an act, or mode of action. This is problematic since unity of nature precedes any of these activities or properties. Tertullian's emphasis on the Divine as Spirit, which is a nature not a person (Spirit as equivalent to substance), seems to suggest that Spirit is that substance which is common to all the members of the Divine community.[54] As we find in John 4, "God is Spirit." In the African worldview, Spirit is the basis of all that there is, including the gods. Spirit also has the capacity for interpenetration. If all the members of the Divine community partake in the spiritual nature of Divinity, it is not impossible for them to penetrate and indwell one another. The equality of the members is grounded in the fact that the Divine is Spirit.

According to deMagerie, spiritual beings, genuinely constituted on the level of substances or nature in their "inseity" of the soul and body, are nevertheless situated in the world by a complex of accidental relations of dependence, of dynamisms and subordinations that coordinate them with others.[55] For other beings, such as humanity, their spiritual beings allow them to be codeterminant of their being but the Divine is that Spirit that determines materiality and all other modes of being, as well as its own being. The Divine is capable of interpenetrating not only Spirit, but all natures. This, of course, is consistent with the African emphasis on spirits. But there are various spirits and the Spirit of the Divine being is separate and greater than the spirit of humanity or other spirits, yet it encompasses all.

Tertullian also introduced the doctrine of relations into the trinitarian theology by emphasizing the relationality of Father and Son, and by extension, the relation of the Holy Spirit to the two. The doctrine of the distinction of persons in the Trinity is based on interpersonal relationship. The vitality common to the three is Spirit and form the basis of the Divine nature. This vitality permits the Divine in-itself and for-itself to leave intact the relative aspect of the with-respect-to-others by which the members of the Divine community are distinguished. The *relation to another does not* result in the loss of their identity. According to deMargerie, when relation is applied to the intimate life of the Divine community as a way to explain distinction within unity, it permits us to defend vigorously the perfect equality of the Divine person, not by elimination or nominality, but by actual distinction of persons.[56] Tertullian is quite clear that this distinction is "not only by the mention of names as Father, Son, [and Holy Ghost]" but by the presence of different personifying identities capable of taking on specific functions, without effecting a severance or division within the Divine Community.[57]

NOTES

1. See generally Leonard E. Elliot-Binns, *The Beginning of Western Christendom* (Greenwich, Conn.: Seabury Press, 1957).
2. Ibid., 142–62.
3. Peter C. Hodgson, *God in History: Shapes of Freedom* (Nashville: Abingdon,

1989), 14.
4. Ibid.
5. Lipsius, *Zietschrift fur wissenschaftliche Theologie,* (1866), 194, cited by Benjamin B. Warfield, *Studies in Tertullian and Augustine* (Westport, Conn.: Greenwood Press, 1970), 16.
6. Quintus S. F. Tertullian, *Adversus Praxeas,* trans. Peter Holmes, hereafter cited as *Ad. Praxeas,* in James Roberts and James Donaldson, eds., *Ante-Nicene Fathers,* vol. 3 (Grand Rapids, Mich.: Wm. B. Eerdmans Publishers, 1951). All references to the work of Tertullian in English are from this work unless otherwise stated. References in Latin are taken from Q. S. F. Tertullianus, *Adversus Praxean Ad* Fidem Editionvm Aem Kroymann et Ernest Evans, (Edited by Kroymann and Ernest Evans) in *Corpvs Christianorvm* (The Christian Corpus), series Latina 2 (Turnholti, Italy: Typographi Brepolis Editores Pontificii, 1954), unless otherwise stated.
7. *Ad. Praxeas,* ch. 12, 606.
8. *Ad. Praxeas,* ch. 12.
9. *Ad. Praxeas,* ch. 7.
10. Ibid.
11. *Ad. Praxeas,* ch. 6, 601.
12. *Ad. Praxeas,* ch. 6.
13. *Ad. Praxeas,* ch. 12.
14. *Ad. Praxeas,* ch. 12.
15. Betrand deMargerie, *The Christian Trinity in History,* trans. Edmund J. Fortmann (Stillriver, Miss.: Saint Bede's Publication, 1982), 78.
16. Tertullian, *De Baptismo,* in *Ante-Nicene Fathers,* ch. 6.
17. deMargerie, 62.
18. *Ad. Praxeas,* ch. 2.
19. *Ad. Praxeas,* ch. 2.
20. Warfield, 24.
21. Ibid., 25.
22. *Ad. Praxeas,* ch. 7. See also deMargerie, 80.
23. deMargerie, 80.
24. *Ad. Praxeas,* ch. 5.
25. *Ad. Praxeas,* ch. 8.
26. Ibid.
27. Ibid.
28. Ibid.
29. Ibid.
30. *Ad. Praxeas,* ch. 2.
31. *Ad. Praxeas,* ch. 3.
32. *Ad. Praxeas,* ch. 3.
33. Ibid. This may indicate that his native language was not Latin or Greek. These were languages of the conquerors.
34. Ibid.
35. Ibid.
36. Ibid.
37. Ibid.
38. The term kingdom or community is a more fitting representation of what Tertullian seems to be conveying by the term monarchy or community

of rulers. This more aptly represents what might have transpired among the African indiginous peoples with regards to leadership by a group of elders, represented by one power but with diverse functional authority.

39. *Ad, Praxeas,* ch. 5.
40. *Ad. Praxeas,* ch. 7.
41. *Ad. Praxeas,* ch. 7.
42. See *Ad. Praxeas,* Chaps. 5 and 6.
43. See Bishop Bull, "Definition of Nicene Creed," Oxford translation, in Roberts *The Ante-Nicene Fathers,* 2:516. Pages
44. Jean Danielou, *A History of Early Church Doctrine.* vol. 3 of *The Origins of Latin Christianity,* trans. David Smith and John Baker, (Philadelphia: Westminster Press, 1977), 366.
45. Danielou, 364–66.
46. *Ad. Praxeas,* ch. 5.
47. Ibid., ch. 2.
48. Ibid.
49. Ibid.
50. Ibid.
51. See also *Ad. Praxeas,* ch. 2.
52. Edmund J. Fortmann, *The Triune God: A Historical Study of the Doctrine of the Trinity* (Grand Rapids, Mich: Baker Book House, 1972), xix.
53. These illustrations are listed above. Or see *Ad. Praxeas,* ch. 2.
54. *Ad. Praxeas,* ch. 5.
55. deMargerie, 80.
56. deMargerie, 138.
57. *Ad. Praxeas,* 4.

Five

IMAGES EXPRESSIVE OF RELATIONAL INTERPLAY WITHIN THE DIVINE COMMUNITY

In looking at Tertullian's work on the Trinity, one notices a curious dialectical balance of metaphors that are at play with one another. If one takes each metaphor in isolation, without seeking for that with which it is at play, the sense of communality might be missed. In expressing the relational interplay within the Divine community, Tertullian creates a certain sense of *juissance terminologique*. In such playful dialectic, terms such as *substance* will have to be defined in their relational milieu. Hence, a word such as substance does not stand alone in Tertullian's thought, but stands in relation to other words or particular situations. In the case of the Trinity, the word substance is related to particular persons within Community. Several of the words-at-play will be used within this chapter as a way to elucidate the communal element in Tertullian's Divinity.

SUBSTANCE AND PERSON

According to Bertrand deMargerie, the Latin translation of the Greek *hypostasis* is *substantiae*. *Substantiae* is used by Tertullian to indicate the idea that the Trinity as a whole is consubstantial with each member—the Father, the Son, and the Holy Spirit. Although, in Tertullian's schema, the Father as Father cannot be, and is not generated by the Son in the course of historical-economic manifestation, they are nonetheless "consubstantial in that they subsist conjointly in the same numerically single nature and substance, in which persons (*prosopon*) are identified within that single nature, though not identical."[1] While in reality it is difficult to establish a distinction between person and nature, there is still a distinction between the function of the person and the nature of the species to which that nature is common. This is the kind of distinction that Tertullian appears to make.

Substance, in fact, seems to point to a dynamic, organic unity, not in terms of particular material manifestations but in relation to the source, as opposed to mathematical atomistic unity. Substance, in Tertullian's usage is, Spirit, which is organic and plurifiable, not mono-personalistic and static. The term *substance* is analogous to, but not exhausted by the notion of unity that deals with communal identity in the sense of moral nature.[2] The community then, is one in the sense of *unitas in substantia*.

Unitas when used by Tertullian in reference to doctrine does not mean that there is a single doctrine. His work shows that he accepts the existence of bodies of propositions regarding various doctrines. *Unitas* refers to the spirit of doctrine as one. This is precisely because the Propositions proceed from the same source and have as their goal the sanctification of humanity. Thus, when Tertullian connects *unitas* with substance, the reference is not to a single being in terms of a single person, or even to a single person manifesting oneself in various forms, but to that which pervades and reaches beyond a single entity to include others in its oneness. In the use of the term *unitas,* one finds the communal principle at work in Tertullian's conception of God.

In Tertullian's view, God is not merely a single object or a process called constructive integration, which has the unique property of existing in the three total but distinctive presentations.[3] For him, the doctrine of God as formulated as one *ousia* in three (*hypostasis*) does not mean "that God, regarded from the point of view of internal analysis, is one object, but that, regarded from the point of view of external presentation, God is three objects.[4] God's unity is not safeguarded by the doctrine that these three as one object are identically one, but that they are indeed three objects with a common subjectivity.[5] We encounter a problem because our concept of oneness hinders us from dealing with the problem of internal or immanent distinction within the Godhead. Tertullian never says the object is one (*unus*), but are one (*unum*). Substance as he uses it in reference to the Divine community is not an object but a force, a pervasive guiding principle for a particular mode of being.

Christopher Stead, commenting on the use of substance in Tertullian, argues that Tertullian's use of the term is indeed non-Aristotelian.[6] He notes correctly that Tertullian seldom mentions Aristotle except for the purpose of denouncing him. Since the concept of the primacy of the individual is very Aristotelian, Tertullian as an African and coming from

an African worldviews with its assumption of the primacy of the community would have had difficulty accepting Aristotelian *proto ousia* as the
basis of the Divine community.[7] In fact, after considering various uses of
the term in Tertullian's work on the Trinity, Stead concludes that with
the sparse use of Aristotelian concepts and terms, Aristotle "can hardly
be determinative in his [Tertullian's] use of *substantia*.[8]

The word *substantia,* as Stead finds it in Tertullian, could have several
meanings. But Stead chooses to argue that it means "the unique stuff
which is or composes the Divine corpus and which Tertullian denotes
spiritus as the way to talk about the Divine."[9]

According to Stead, Tertullian rejects the Stoic use of *substantia* in
reference to the stuff or material of which it is made.[10] But Stead in his
analysis of the term argues that, while *substantia* can mean a single
individual being, Tertullian's use of the term is to be taken to represent
the Spirit, which is God and in which the members of the Divine community share.[11] Stead, then, while accepting that in the Aristotelian sense,
substance can mean a single thing, rejects its application to Tertullian's
theory of Divinity. Stead concludes his work by maintaining that "Tertullian's use of the term may possibly accept, but did not intend, the interpretation put upon it by Western Theology."[12] What then did it intend? Indeed,
it did intend the communality of the Divine.

In Tertullian's case, substance came to be interchangeable with nature
(not *natura,* which referred to physical nature or the natural universe),
but to the "Divine stuff" or the "human stuff." Wolfson points out that
there are three senses in which the term could have been used in Tertullian.

> It may have been used as the conventionalized translation of the Greek
> term *ousia,* in which case the term could not have been used in the
> sense of Aristotelian first *ousia,* namely in the sense of the individual.
> It could have been used only either as *ousia* in the Aristotelian sense
> of a second *ousia,* that is, specific genus, or as *ousia* in its Stoic
> sense, that is, as the equivalent of the non-proximate *hypokeimenon,*
> namely substratum.[13]

Even if "unity of substance" is taken in its Stoic sense of "unity of
substratum," the concept reemphasizes the idea that the members of Tertullian's Divine community are not mere aggregates who happen to come
together, but conveys the sense of fundamental connectedness not defined
by function but by belonging. For Tertullian, as for the African worldviews
considered previously, this stuff is not static but dynamic and generative.

Though Tertullian does use the term *substance* in many ways, for example, in *De Exhortaione Castitas,* his most consistent use of the term *substantia* can be equated with essence as distinguished from function or various historical activities and appearances.[14] As has been noted, the term *being* is connected to *substance* (as in nature) with a fundamental, ontological, relational principle that makes it possible for the members to be called God (that which makes an entity Divine) as it relates to the Divine community. If we refer to *substance* as a single being, we risk making *substance* an entity rather than a force. Such an interpretation will not be consistent with Tertullian. The "ness" in Godness is a relational principle.

The fact that Tertullian uses the word *essentia* sometimes interchangeably with *substantia* seem to suggest that the term *substance,* when used in reference to the Godhead, does not refer to a single being. In *Deus Christianorum,* Rene Braun rejects the idea that Tertullian's use of the term is borrowed directly from the language of Roman jurisprudence. Braun maintains this position in counteraction to Adolf Von Harnack. Regarding Harnack's position, Braun has this to say, *"Il avait exagere le sense juridique de substantia qui n'jamais constitue dans l'esprit des juristes, un categorie nette et distincte."*[15] [he exagerated the legal Sense of Substance which is not a clearly articulated concept in the thought of the jurists] Braun also criticizes Ernest Evans for maintaining that Tertullian's use of the term is strictly related to an Aristotelian notion of a single entity or thing.[16] In contraposition to all of these, Braun contends that while Tertullian uses the term to refer to particular concrete things, *"mais Tertullien n'ignore pas d'autres signification que nous avon reconnue aux origines meme de l'application philosophique du terme: celle de ≪nature≫ et celle de ≪realite≫."*[17] [But Tertullian also does not ignore the signification which we have acknowledged as the original use of the term: that of "nature" and that of "reality".]

As has already been seen in Wolfson's argument, if one is looking for a strictly Aristotelian notion of substance in Tertullian's conception of the Divine community, one is bound to be confused. In Tertullian's work, *substance* is indeed the "monistic principle of relatedness."[18] However, this is not a principle that humanity is capable of knowing independent of its personifications. Indeed, the idea of *substance* in Tertullian seems to function as that which correlates the permanence of the Divine nature with the fact of Divine interaction with the world, particularly in the realm of Divine *probole* (becoming or emanations) in which the Son becomes, from the Father and the Holy Spirit, while the Holy Spirit becomes both from the Father and the Son, and the Father is not the Father without the Son and the Holy Spirit and none of them will be Divine if they were not Spirit. This *substance* in Tertullian is the conditio sine qua non for the unity of variety within the Divine community. Not even the later concept of interpenetration—*perichoresis*—which as we have seen is compatible with the African concept and emphasis on Spirit (or Force which is capable of being penetrated as well as penetrating) of the members of the Divine community reduces the members to mere reflections of the other. The *substance* is that which keeps the variety from being the basis of complete separation. Again this calls to mind Tertullian's idea that Wisdom and Reason within God are real members of the Divine community, not abstractions, for according to Tertullian that which is in God cannot be without corporeal reality. So, it is possible for God to be in Wisdom, as well as Wisdom to be in God without "spiritness" or *substance*.

The fact that Tertullian is attacking Monarchian theory of the Divine as a single personal being should discourage the translation of the term, as he uses it in reference to the Divine community, to mean an entity or single personal being. In *De Anima,* Tertullian uses the term *natura* in the same sense as *substantia,* is being used in reference to that which makes the persons of the God community one.[19] We also find similar use of the term *substantia* in reference to the nature of idolatry not as a property attached to a thing that is also possessed by the individual thing, but that which determines to what class of being the particular thing in consideration belongs. For example, in *De Idolatria* Tertullian says, *"in illa mendicium, cum tota substantia eius mendax sit."*[20] The same use is found in *De Idolatris* 2:1, denoting a particular character or specific behavior trait, as is the case when Tertullian says, *"sufficit sibi tam inimicum deo nomen tam locuples substantia criminis* [A name, so hostile to God and substance so rife with crime is sufficient to itself]."[21] This also shows that *substantia* points to something that is shared in common by several particulars.

Substance is also used by Tertullian in connection to *unitas* as seen in the statement *"una substantia tres persona."* (one substance three persons) *Unitas et Trinitas* (Unity and Trinity) can be placed parallel in Tertullian, thus, *unitas* is connected to *substantia* while *tres persona* should be Connected, to the *Trinitas.* In *Adversus Praxeas,* Tertullian refers to the unity of God twelve times and yet all the while arguing that he does not mean a single personal being, but a One—Unum consisting of Many.[22]

Substance can be defined as that which is a necessary part of the definition of what it means to be God. We may not be able to find an example of this in Greek philosophy, but we may in African cosmology.

In the *Apology,* Tertullian has argued against non-Christian theology that the Divine is multiple—that there are many Gods divided ontologically and functioning on different spheres without a basic relational unifying principle. He insisted on the absolute oneness of God, which he then has to explain later in opposition to singularity. In the Apology Tertullian seems to argue the other extreme that God is one in a way that precludes communality. But that seeming extreme is corrected in *Adversus Praxeas.*

UNITY AND DIVERSITY

The term *unitas,* to which the term *substantia* seems to be connected in Tertullian, apparently refers to the unifying force that crosses the boundary of individual particularity—to that which is common among the species—the Vital Force. Tertullian expressly says that the members of the Divine community are not divided in power. This is closer to the African concept of the Divine than may be thought at first glance. Placid Temples has shown that fundamental to the African worldview is the concept of vital force, which is capable of generating or multiplying itself infinitely both in its individual presence and in its general sense.[23]

The idea that realms of beings can be multiplied or diminished arbitrarily, depending on one's frame of reference, has been advanced by Edgar Brightman. However, it does not seem that substratic principles guiding particular modes of being can be multiplied indefinitely.[24] If one's frame of reference is relational—as in the traditional African's or Tertullian's— the number of relationships can increase ad infinitum unless some tradition places boundaries; Tertullian's conviction was that his position of revealed truth frees him to stop such increase. In Tertullian's case, the Christian revelation of the *substance.* If one posits a separated substance as a basis for relationality thus creating a view of static substantiality, unaffected by internal or external relationality, a multiplicity of beings or persons will be logically difficult, but still not impossible. But "substance is needed both as ground of permanence and as a ground of change."[25] *Substance* depends not only on its own past but also on the interaction and communication with entities emerging from it that continually alter and enrich it and through which it is know. Either way, whether the substance of Tertullian is seen as fully dwelling in the Father and begetting the rest or seen as the essential emerging basis of all the entities including the Father, the substance is enriched, nonetheless, by its interaction with the related entities. In fact, Tertullian relationalizes *substance* in both senses.

According to Brightman, a clear concept of substantial permanence requires the concept of continuous duration. *Substance* is inseparably related to continuity, in fact it is causal continuity. The concept of *substance,* in other words, is bare and empty, needing to fulfill itself by constantly becoming full of personhood through which it is known. *Substance* cannot be known except in its becoming.[26] *Substance* is thus the active principle of relations among entities of common species and the causal efficacious force of being in the process of becoming.

The term *persona* used by Tertullian helped to express this concept of diversity. Tertullian intended to maintain the unity, as well as the diversity within the God community. Tertullian, in arguing against Praxeas, and using the phrase, *"Una substantia tres persona"* to underscore the idea that God-community has one essence, nature or substance that is shared by the Father, the Son, and the Holy Spirit, developed a radical new way of consceiving God based on African Communality. He also preserved Divine personaties by maintaining that they share the same ontological nature, but their distinctiveness is real and actual. This nature that they share is not a personal entity in and of itself, though it is capable of personification. Any community deserving the name must have some sense of connection even in diversity.

Tertullian also uses the word *status* in relation to *substance* to show that the three belong to the same class. But this *status* should not be confused with static; it is rather a definition of belonging to the same category of being. This *status* should be understood in terms of standing within—in relation to. This allows Tertullian to argue that there is only one Divine nature while still maintaining its internal diversification into three actual entities. Within this one nature are three things, three entities: the first one who maybe regarded as father, the *ratio* (intellect) or *sermo* (seed), which was another and second the Holy Spirit who is yet another. The Holy spirit is to be distinguished from the fact that the *substance* that is shared by the three is Spirit, for "God is Spirit." This Spirit seems to be the gathering force of the total economic experience of the members of the Godhead.[27] The *substance* then is the basis of equality within the community of the Divine that keeps the distinction from being ontologically subordinate, while the persons are the basis for all economic interactions.

POWER AND AUTHORITY

In every community there is a constant battle as to the relation of power and authority. Dealing with the Divine as community raises the issue of the locus of power and the source of authority. The question of substance helps Tertullian to solve this dilemma because Tertullian connects it with the idea of power and nature. How can they have one Power unless this power is communal in nature? Power is thus not seen as the possession of a singular individual within the Divine community. Rather, power, like substance and nature, belongs to the unchangeable and essential nature of what it means to be Divine. The danger one finds in Tertullian is the possibility of calling the *substance* God in such a way that it becomes a God apart from the three persons. However, by maintaining that this *substance,* though invisibly hidden in the Father, is at the same time shared by the three on the ontological level (and making it a force) and removing it from the clutch of personalism, Tertullian seems to avoid this problem.

One cannot know this *substance* except as it reveals itself in particular members of the Divine community. This is not so removed from the African view that the impersonal pervading force that inhabits the gods cannot be known directly except as it is manifested in particular gods. This mode of looking at it, underscores the ignorance of those who ask Africans: Do you know the supreme principle? Of course, they do not, and nobody does. This, for the African, is like asking one whether they know the whole universe directly. They know the universe as it is particularized in their presence. A more correct question then becomes: How do you know this substance or power? Yet, the problem remains as to why this force can only manifest itself in three. Is this limitation inherent in the community of the Godhead or the result of revelation? It seems that, for Tertullian as a Christian, the limit is imposed by his acceptance of a tradition of scriptural interpretation that interprets the Divine as three.

Tertullian uses the term *gradus* (degree) and the term *persona* in relation to the economic Trinity, which may seem to belie the contention in this chapter of equality of nature and hence of power. This is not necessarily the case. The economy is the historical manifestation of the persons within the God community as it moves in its relation to the created order. These terms seem to be the basis of the cosmological Trinity in Tertullian. It is in connection to these terms that we find the emphasis on subordination in his thought. In the idea of the economy in relation to the objective creation of the cosmos, the God community is externalized. In the process of this externalization, the Divine community is subordinated.

The economy is a manifestation of more than just the acts of the persons within the God community; it shows the immanence of the three within that community. The act of creation in the Historical manifestation of the Trinity is not necessitated in such a way that it determines all their ontology as God. For example, if God did not create, would God still be God? Tertullian thinks so in his argument against Homogenes. Rather, it is precisely by virtue of the shared ontology, the fact of sharing the Divine nature or substance, that the members of the Divine community can act in relation to the economy or historical epochs of the cosmos. What determines the particular form which the act of a member may take is not ontological but historical, and the connection to history, though real, is temporal. Because they are ontologically equal there is no second and no third, no degrees of Godhood. They share the same substance, power, and nature. This I believe is what Tertullian means to convey by the statement *Tres Unum est no unus.* When he says, *"Una substantia tres persona,"* it may be understood in dual relationality between members of the community, as well as their relation to the created order, while *una substantia* is to be understood mainly in terms of their relationality within the Godhead and how their relation results in relationship to the world.

Tertullian's Trinity was more pluralistic than that of other Theologians who were his contemporaries. Tertullian's contemporaries recognized this and charged him with proclaiming three Gods.* If one will argue (as has been done by some) that the Father is the whole substance and that Tertullian returned to monotheism by making the Father the fullest of the three, one will also have to take into consideration the places where Tertullian argues that the other two are "the power and entire system of the monarchy."[28] How they can be the "power and the entire system" can only be understood if each member of the Divine community is seen as God who shares in the fullness of the substance, even in their particularity.

The concept of a shared power, which is one for all, is also evidenced in Tertullian's rejection of ontological subordination within the Divine community. This does not necessarily imply a complete rejection of all manner of authority and responsibility distributed hierarchically. The rejection of what Jean Danielou calls "angelmorphic Christology" is an example of this. Such a position holds that since one member of the community

* note: See Ad. Praxeas ch. 1.

chooses to serve in a certain capacity such as savior, that member must be naturally inferior to the others, or why else will they choose to serve? Tertullian by arguing for oneness of substance rejects this supposition. Danielou is correct in stating that

> this idea of Christ as an envoy and an angel does not appear at all in Tertullian's work. This is clearly evidence of the fact that he [Tertullian] was anxious to avoid all cause of confusion between the Son [as generated within the Godhead Having real kinship with the father] and the angels [who are created not generated]. . . .[29]

The so-called angelmorphic or created Divinity will seem to support ontological subordination. There were those who said, according to Tertullian, that Gen. 1:1 should be read *"In principio Deus fecit Filium"* (In the beginning God created for himself a son).[30] Even this is rejected by Tertullian, insofar as it implied a difference in fundamental nature.

Tertullian's reaction against the other two views of the Divine community also supports the anti-ontological subordinationist tendency. Another view was one which saw the Divine mainly in terms of single person. This position as represented by Praxeas refused to make any distinction between the members of the Divine community. This is monarchial monotheism in the form of modalism.

There is a second model of the community of the Divine that Tertullian seems to be reacting against in his works, particularly in *Ad Praxeas,* which is the separationist concept of the community. This concept sees the community as atomistic. Against this, Tertullian coined the phrase "different but not separate." Such separation then in the thought of Tertullian will be problematic.

The *substance,* which is shared among the entities called gods, points to the fact that being is understood dynamically as a fundamentally active principle in the universe of the gods. Unless these entities called gods shared in full the power, which is that force that is fundamental to the universe, their Godness will be valueless. The power of the universe, which is not person but *substance,* will not be known except through the personifyings of these beings called gods or other entities.

From Tertullian's work we find that power is one thing shared among the members of the Divine community. However, he never seems to confuse this with the idea that one member functions, for example, as the substitutionary sacrifice for the sins of the world or that the Holy

Spirit teaches or reveals new dimensions of Christ's work. These functions do not make these members of the Divine community inferior in nature. It is precisely this power that makes their activities valid and efficacious. The sharing of this power seems connected to Tertullian's idea of *substance,* a commonality that itself supports the idea of equality. The members of the Divine community are plural, not in status (order of divinity), but in *gradus* (degree of emergence and responsibility); not in *substance* but in persons, not in power but in aspects of the uses of that power (authority). They are of one substance, one status, and of one power, three grades, three persons, three aspects of uses of power and distributive responsibility.

EQUALITY AND SUBORDINATION

The concept of equality in community is tied to substance, nature, and power. There are no degrees (*gradus*) of Godhood. There is one order of being God. All the members of the Divine community, by virtue of their inner connection that one order of being God, and embodying that principle of being, are naturally equal. The arguments, therefore, which have been advanced for the concept of *substance* should serve also for the concept of equality. And indeed there is no community, whether human or Divine, which is not ordered with varieties of responsibilities, but when these varieties of responsibilities are used to determine Ontological inferiority and superiority it becomes a problem. It is these varieties of responsibilities which engender subordination.

In the Divine community, then, there is subordination. This subordination is historical and temporal. Historical-temporal-functional subordination is not the same as natural, substantial, or ontological subordination in the thought of Tertullian. The term *historical* is used because something can manifest historicity without being temporal. Temporality is a term used here for the purpose of clarity. It denotes the dynamic and open-ended nature of functions, which persons undertake in a particular mode of being. In the Divine community, the Son, by virtue of being Son, acquires a functionally subordinate status, but not an ontologically-natural-ly-entropic inferior-subordination.[31] This concept of the Divine Community as developed within African Worldview and the thought of Tertullian protests the Concept of Communal Belonging and Connection without sacrificing individuality. Within African Worldview Fatherhood, Motherhood Sonship, daughtership is a temporal-functional phenomenon. A father is not a father always. The idea of Spiritual pre-existence in a State of

Spiritual equality-de-ontologizes the concept of father or mother. In African world then there is a sense in which that one who child today in the future becomes parent of that one who is parent today. Fatherhood or childhood does not remove the fundamental humanity of either persons fulfilling those specific functions. One is not ontological inferior just because one is child-son, daughter of grand child.

NOTES

1. deMargerie, 131.
2. Rene Braun, *Deus Christianorum: Recherches sur le vocabulaire doctrinal de Tertullien* [Research on the doctrinal vocabulary of Tertullian] (Paris: Etudes Augustiniennes, 1977), 90.
3. George L. Prestige, *God in Patristic Thought* (London: SPCK, 1952), 97–111.
4. Ibid.
5. Ibid.
6. Stead, 48, 51, and 54.
7. Christopher Stead, 54. See also Harry Austyn Wolfson, *The Philosophy of the Church Fathers* (Cambridge: Harvard University Press, 1970), 324 An example of this usage which occurs in Quintillian's *Institutio Oratio* II, 15, 34.
8. Stead, 57.
9. Stead, 63.
10. Ibid., 50.
11. Stead, 48, 51, and 63.
12. Ibid., 51.
13. Wolfson, *The Philosophy of the Church fathers* 325.
14. See also Stead, 48.
15. Braun, 178.
16. Ibid., 179.
17. Ibid., 180.
18. Edgar Sheffield Brightman, *Person and Reality: Introduction to Metaphysics,* ed. Peter A. Bertocci, (New York: Roland Press, 1958), 86.
19. Tertullian, *De Anima,* ch. 32 in *Ante Nicene Fathers,* eds. J. Robert and J. Donaldson.
20. Tertullian, *De Idolatria,* in *Corpvs Chritianorvm,* Series latina (Turnholti, Italy: Typographi Brepolis Editores Pontifici, 1954) eds. Aem Kroymann and Ernest Evans 1:4.
21. Ibid., ch. 2.
22. Braun, 142.
23. See Braun, also Placido Temple, 162.
24. Brightman, *Bantu Philosophy,* 91.
25. Ibid., 111.
26. Ibid.
27. Tertullian speaks of immanent Trinity without resorting to the theory of eternal generation of the son. Novatian thought that the only way to explain the equality of the son to the father was to argue the eternal generation of the son, yet he seems not to see that eternal generation sets up an eternal subordination

and makes the son eternally unequal to the father, similarity of nature not withstanding. See Novatian, *The Trinity* in *The Fathers of the Church,* 67. Trans. Russell J. DeSimone (Washington, D. C.: Catholic University of America Press, 1974).
28. *Ad. Praxeas,* ch. 5.
29. Danielou, 102. See also Tertullian's *De Carne Christi* in *Ante-Nicene Fathers.*
30. *Ad. Praxeas,* 5.
31. This is the basis, I believe, of the failure of some Gnostic systems such as Valentinus' which allowed for basic inner ontological structural subordination within the Divine community, and led to the entropization of nature and hence inferiority (which was not mainly functional but also ontological). Not surprisingly, it led in many gnostic circles to the separation between the "spiritually" enlightened and the ignorant and even to the perception that some human begins are created inferior to others as we see in Origen. The reason for this injustice is sought for in a pre-corporeal state of existence which is supposed to be far superior to the present human forms.

Epilogue

From the African perspective communality, indeed, is the essence of the gods in African worldviews. In the Africa of ancient Egypt, the triadic concept reveals this communality. The Trinity as developed by Tertullian, affirms it. In today's Africa, the concepts of generativity among the gods and fundamental relationality underscore communality. Since communality and relationality are fundamental in African worldviews, the concept of the Divine communality is not only logical but also necessary. All such a concept which do not take this communality into consideration are irrelevant.

This communality of the Divine is a community of equality. This equality is based on the fact that all share in one nature. Though the members share in one substance their are actuality as persons is not compromised. The members of the Divine community are all embodiments of that supreme all-pervasive force that is their substance. Substance is a dynamic generative principle.

Relationality is also a basic characteristic of the Divine community. The gods or the persons within the Divine community are not separated from one another, rather they are connected as members of the same family.

Traditional African religions, whether in ancient Egypt, in modern Africa or in Tertullian's African Christianity, do not conceive of the Divine in monotheistic or separetionistic terms. Since singularistic personal monotheism precludes intrinsic relationality, it is, in fact, contrary to communal interactiveness. Separationism, which is an irreconcilable duality as expressed by Marcion, also fails to do justice to the concept of communality in the African worldview. The conception of the Divine in these three African contexts is communal, and the gods, because of their fundamental relations, are seen as equal both in power and nature. This concept of shared nature and power disallows ontological subordination.

But every idea of the Divine raises some very important questions for human community. The idea of the Divine community raises such questions as: What kind of human patterns of interaction within community should be envisioned? How will the human community look if modeled after the Divine community? What will be the criteria for belonging to such community?

The issues of substance and economy call forth the problems of persons within community of the question of equality and subordination, and of freedom and participation.

Bibliography

AFRICAN RELIGION

Alabe, Thomas Sube. *Religion in Bakossi Traditional Society: A Literary Inquiry.* Yaounde, Cameroon: Alabe, 1979.

Allen, James P. *Genesis in Egypt: The Philosophy of Ancient Egyptian Creation Account.* New Haven Conn.: Yale University Press, 1988.

Arinze, Francis A. *Sacrifice in Ibo Religion.* Edited J. S. Boston. Ibadan, Nigeria: Ibadan University Press, 1970.

Asante, Molefi Kete. *The Afrocentric Idea.* Philadelphia: Temple University Press, 1987.

Barnes, Sandra T., ed. *Africa's Ogun: Old World and New.* Bloomington: Indiana University Press, 1989.

Beattie, John, and John Middleton. *Spirit Mediumship and Society in Africa.* New York: Africana Publishing, 1969.

Bell, William Clark. *African Bridge Builders.* New York: Friendship Press, 1936.

Binsbergen, Wim Van, and Matthew Schoffeleers, eds. *Theoretical Explorations in African Religion.* London: KPI, 1985.

Boulnois, Jean. *Gnon-Gua Dueu des Curiere.* Paris: Fourmer, 1933.

Breasted, James Henry. *A History of Egypt: From the Earliest Time to the Persian Conquest.* New York: Charles Scribner's Sons, 1951.

Buck, Adriaan de. *The Egyptian Coffin Text.* Vol. 2. Chicago: Chicago University Press, 1939.

Budge, E. A. Wallis. *The Book of the Dead.* New Hyde Park, N.Y.: University Books, 1960.

Christensen, Thomas G. *An African Tree of Life.* Maryknoll, N.Y.: Orbis Books, 1990.

Clark, R. T. Rundle. *Myth and Symbol in Ancient Egypt.* New York: Grove Press, 1960.

Cole, Herbert M. *Mbari: Art and Life Among the Owerri Igbo.*
Bloomington: Indiana University Press, 1982.
Danquah, Joseph B. *The Akan Doctrine of God.* London: Lutterworth
Press, 1944.
Deng, Francis Mading. *Dinka Cosmology.* London: Ithaca Press, 1980.
Dickson, Kwesi A. *Theology in Africa.* Maryknoll, N.Y.: Orbis
Books, 1984.
Dickson, Kwesi A., and Paul Ellingworth. *Biblical Revelation and
African Beliefs.* Maryknoll, N.Y.: Orbis Books, 1969.
Dine, George Uchechukwu. *Traditional Leadership as Service Among
the Igbos of Nigeria.* Rome: Pont University Lataranense,
1983.
Ela, Jean Marc. *My Faith as an African.* Translated by John P. Brown
and Susan Perry. Maryknoll, N.Y.: Orbis Books, 1988.
Erskine, Noe Leo. *Decolonizing Theology.* Maryknoll, N.Y.: Orbis
Books, 1981.
Evans-Pritchard, E. E. *The Nuer: A Description of the Modes of
Livelihood and Political Institutions of a Nilotic People.*
Oxford: Clarendon Press, 1963.
———. *Nuer Religion.* Oxford: Clarendon Press, 1956.
———. *Witchcraft, Oracles and Magic Among the Azande.* Oxford:
Clarendon Press, 1937.
Fernandez, James W. *Bwiti: An Ethnography of Religious Imagination
in Africa.* New York: Princeton University Press, 1982.
Forde, Darryl. *African Worlds.* London: Ward Loce Educational, 1980.
Fowden, Garth. *The Egyptian Hermes.* Cambridge: Cambridge
University Press, 1986.
Gardiner, Alan. *Egypt of the Pharaohs: An Introduction.* Oxford:
Clarendon Press, 1961.
Gennep, Arnold V. *The Rites of Passage.* Translated by Monica B.
Vizedom and Gabrielle L. Caffee. Chicago: University of
Chicago Press, 1960.
Girodani, Igino. *The Social Message of the Early Church Fathers.*
Translated by Alba I. Zizzamia. Patterson, N.J.: St. Anthony
Guild Press, 1944.
Goff, Beatrice L. *Symbols of Ancient Egypt in the Late Period.* New
York: Mouton Publishers, 1979.
Griaule, Marcal. *Dieu d'eau: Entretiens avec Ogotemmeli.* Paris:
Fayard, 1975.

Harjula, Raimo. *God and the Sun in Meru Thought.* Helsinki: Finish Society for Missiology and Ecumenics, 1969.

Herskovits, Frances S., and J. Melville. *Dahomean Narrative: A Cross Cultural Analysis.* Evanston: Northwestern University Press, 1958.

Hopegood, Cecil R. "Conception of God Amongst the Tonga of Zambia," in *African Idea of God.* editor Edwin W. Smith. London: Edinburgh House Press, 1966.

Hornung, Erik. *Conceptions of God in Ancient Egypt: The One and the Many.* Translated by John Baines. Ithaca: Cornell University Press, 1971.

Horton, Robin. *The Gods as Guests: An Aspect of Kalabari Religious Life.* Series 3. Lagos: Nigeria Magazine Publishers, 1960.

Idowu, E. Bolaji. *African Traditional Religion: A Definition.* London: SCM Press, 1973.

————. *Oluodumare: God in Yoruba Belief.* London: Longman Press, 1975.

Illogu, Edmund. *Christianity and Igbo Culture.* Enugu, Nigeria: Nok Publishers, 1974.

Jahn, Janheinz. *Muntu.* Paris: Editions du Seuil, 1958.

Janzen, John M. *Lemba: A Drum of Affliction in Africa and the New World.* New York: Garland Publishing, 1982.

Kroger, Franz. *Ancestor Worship Among the Bulsa of Northern Ghana: Religious Social and Economic Aspects.* Munich: K. Renner, 1982.

Kunene, Mazisi. *Anthem of the Decade.* 1968. Reprint. Ibadan, Nigeria: Heinemann, 1981.

Kunkare, Edward. *The Destiny of Man: Baagarne Beliefs in Dialogue with Christian Escathology.* New York: P. Lang, 1985.

Lamy, Lucie. *Egyptian Mysteries.* New York: Crossroad, 1981.

Leinhardt, R. Godfrey. *Divinity and Experience: The Religion of the Dinka People.* Oxford: Clarendon Press, 1960.

LeMoal, Guy. *Les Bobo: Nature et Function des Masques.* Paris: Orstom, 1980.

Levy-Bruhl, Lucien. *The Soul of the Primitive.* London: George Allen and Unwin, 1965.

MacVeigh, Malcolm J. *God in Africa: Conceptions of God in African Traditional Religion and Christianity.* Cape Cod, Mass.: C. Stark, 1974.

Maxwell, Kevin B. *Bemba Myth and Ritual: The Impact of Literacy on an Oral Culture.* New York: Plang, 1983.

Mbiti, John. *African Religion and Philosophy.* New York: Praeger, 1969.

————. *Concepts of God in Africa.* New York: Praeger Publishers, 1970.

Metuh, Emefie Ikenga. *God and Man in African Religion: A Case Study of the Igbo of Nigeria.* London: G. Chapman, 1981.

————. "The Supreme God in Igbo Life and Worship." *Journal of Religion in Africa* 1 (May 1973): 20–42.

Moore, Basil, ed. *The Challenge of Black Theology in South Africa.* Atlanta: John Knox Press, 1973.

Morenz, Sigfreid. *Egyptian Religion.* Translated by Ann E. Keep. London: Methuen and Co., 1973.

Mosala, Itumeleng J., and Buti Tihagale. *The Unquestionable Right to be Free.* Maryknoll, N.Y.: Orbis Books, 1986.

Nadel, Siegried F. *Nupe Religion.* London: Routledge and Kegan Paul, 1954.

Nguema-olsan, Paulin. *Aspects de la Religion Fang.* Paris: Akct Karthala, 1983.

Oduyoye, Modupe. *The Vocabulary of Yoruba Religious Discourse.* Ibadan, Nigeria: Daystar Press, 1971.

Paris, Peter J. *The Social Teaching of the Black Churches.* Philadelphia Fortress Press, 1985.

Parrinder, Geoffrey. *Africa's Three Religions.* London: Sheldon Press, 1976.

————. *West African Religion: A Study of the Belief and Practices of the Akan, Ewe, Yoruba, I[g]bo, and Kindred Peoples.* 1949. Reprint. London: Epworth Press, 1977.

p'Bitek, Okot. *The Religion of the Central Luo.* Nairobi: East African Literature Bureau, 1971.

Ray, Benjamin C. *African Religions Symbol, Ritual, and Community.* Englewood Cliffs, N.J.: Prentice-Hall, 1976.

Read, F. W. *Egyptian Religion and Ethics.* London: Watts and Co., 1925.

Ross, Emory. *African Heritage.* New York: Friendship Press, 1952.

Sawyer, Harry. *God, Ancestor or Creator? Aspects of Traditional Belief in Ghana, Nigeria and Sierra Leone.* Harlow, England: Longman, 1970.

Seligman, C. G. "Multiple Souls in Negro Africa," In *Ancient Egypt.*
3 (1915): 103–11.

Sernett, Milton C., ed. *Afro-American Religious History: A
Documentary Witness.* Durham: Duke University Press,
1985.

Shelton, Austin J. *The Igbo-Igala Borderland: Religion and Social
Control in Indigenous Africa Colonialism.* New York: Albany
State University Press, 1971.

Smith, Edwin E. "A Note On Mulungu," in *African Idea of God,*
Edited by Edwin Smith. London: Edinburgh House Press,
1966.

Sofola, Zulu. "The Theater in the Search for African Authenticity,"
in *African Theology En Route.* Edited by Kofi Appiah-Kubi
and Sergio Torres. Maryknoll, N.Y.: Orbis Books, 1979.

Tarie, G. O. M. *Kalabari Traditional Religion.* Berlin: Reimer,
1977.

Taylor, John V. *The Primal Vision.* London: SCM Press, 1963.

Temples, Placide. *Bantu Philosophy.* Translated by Colin King. Paris:
Presence Africaine, 1959.

Turner, Victor. *The Forest of Symbols: Aspects of Nedlembu Ritual.*
Ithaca, N.Y.: Cornell University Press, 1970.

———. *The Ritual Process: Structure and Anti-Structure.* Chicago:
Aldine, 1969.

Turyabikayo, Rugyema Benoni. *Philosophy and Traditional Religion
of the Baleiga in South West Uganda.* Nairobi: Kenya
Literature Bureau, 1983.

Warren, Henry White. *Among the Forces.* New York: Eaton and
Mains, 1898.

Westerlund, David. *African Religion in African Scholarship: A
Preliminary Study of the Religious and Political Background.*
Stockholm: Almquist and Wiskell, 1985.

Willoughby, W. C. *Nature-Worship and Taboo: Further Studies in
"The Soul of the Bantu."* Hartford Conn.: Hartford Seminary
Press, 1932.

Zahan, Dominique. *The Bambare.* Leiden: Brill, 1974.

Zahan, Dominique. *The Religion, Spirituality, and Thought of
Traditional Africa.* Translated by Kate Ezra Martin and
Lawrence M. Martin. Chicago: University of Chicago Press,
1979.

COMMUNITY

Corrington, Robert S. *The Community of Interpreters.* Macon: Mercer University Press, 1987.

Daly, Herman E., and John B. Cobb. *For the Common Good.* Boston: Beacon Press, 1989.

Hobbes, Thomas. *Leviathan.* Vol 23, *Great Books of the Western World.* Chicago: Encyclopaedia Britannica, 1952.

Kirkpatrick, Frank G. *Community: A Trinity of Models.* Washington, D.C.: Georgetown University Press, 1986.

Leighton, Joseph Alexander. *Man and the Cosmos: An Introduction to Metaphysics.* New York: D. Appleton and Co., 1922.

MacMurray, John. *Persons in Relation* New York: Harper and Bros., 1957.

Oppenheim, Frank. *Royce's Mature Philosophy of Religion.* Notre Dame, Ind.: University of Notre Dame Press, 1987.

Royce, Josiah. *The Problem of Christianity.* Chicago: University of Chicago Press, 1968.

———. "The Problem of Christianity," in *The Philosophy of Josiah Royce.* Edited by John K. Roth. Indianapolis: Hackett Publishing, 1982.

Toennies, Ferdinand. *Community and Society (Gemeinschaft und Gesellschaft).* Translated by Charles P. Loomis. East Lansing: Michigan State University Press, 1957.

PHILOSOPHY

Griffin, David Ray. *God and Religion in a Postmodern World.* Albany, N.Y.: State University of New York Press, 1989.

——— and Houston Smith, *Primordial Truth and Postmodern Theology.* Albany, N.Y.: State University of New York Press, 1989.

Heidegger, Martin. *Being and Time.* Translated by John Macquarrie and Edward Robinson. New York: Harper and Bros., 1962.

Lescoe, Francis J. *Existentialism With or Without God.* New York: Alba House, 1974.

Locke, Don. *Perception and Our Knowledge of the External World.* New York: Humanities Press, 1967.

Magee, John B. *Religion and Modern Man: A Study of the Religious Meaning of Being Human.* New York: Harper and Row, 1967.

Neville, Robert. *The Cosmology of Freedom.* New Haven: Yale University Press, 1974.

Preus, J. Samuel. *Explaining Religion.* New Haven, Conn.: Yale University Press, 1987.

Strasser, Stephan. *The Idea of Dialogical Phenomenology.* Pittsburgh, Pa.: Duquesne University Press, 1969.

Wolfson, Harry Austyn. *The Philosophy of the Church Fathers.* Cambridge: Harvard University Press, 1970.

Young, Henry James. *Hope in Process.* Minneapolis: Fortress Press, 1990.

WORKS BY TERTULLIAN

Tertullianus, Q. S. F. *Adversus Praxean.* Ad Fidem Editionvm Aem Kroymann et Ernest Evans. In *Corpvs Christianorvm* [The Christian Corpus]. Series Latina 2. Turnholt, Belgium: Typographi Brepolis Editores Pontificii, 1954.

Tertullian, Quintus S. F. *Adversus Praxeas.* Translated by Peter Holmes, in James Roberts and James Donaldson, eds. *Ante-Nicene Fathers,* Vol. 3. Grand Rapids Mich.: Wm. B. Eerdmans Publishers, 1951.

———. *Against Marcion.* Translated by Peter Holmes. In James Roberts and James Donaldson eds., *Ante-Nicene Fathers.* Vol. 3. Grand Rapids Mich.: Wm. B. Eerdmans Publishers, 1951.

———. *De Animae.* Translated by Peter Holmes. In James Roberts and James Donaldson eds., *Ante-Nicene Fathers.* Vol. 3. Grand Rapids Mich.: Wm. B. Eerdmans Publishers, 1951.

———. *The Testimony of the Soul.* Translated by Peter Holmes. In James Roberts and James Donaldson eds., *Ante-Nicene Fathers.* Vol. 3. Grand Rapids Mich.: Wm. B. Eerdmans Publishers, 1951.

WORKS ABOUT TERTULLIAN

Braun, Rene. *Deus Christianorum: Recherches sur le vocabulaire doctrinal de Tertullien.* [Research on the doctrinal vocabulary of Tertullian]. Paris: Etudes Augustiniennes, 1977.

Bray, Gerald Lewis. *Holiness and the Will of God.* Atlanta: John Knox Press, 1979.

———. "The Legal Concept Ratio in Tertullian." *Vigilae Christianae* 31 (1977): 94–116.

————. "The Relationship Between Holiness and Chasity in
Tertullian." In *Studia Patristica*. Vol. 16. Edited by E. A.
Livingstone. Berlin: Akademie-Verlag, 1985.

Campenhausen, Hans Von. *The Fathers of the Latin Church.* Translated
by Manfred Hoffman. Stanford: Stanford University Press,
1964.

Church, F. Forrester. "Sex and Salvation in Tertullian." *Harvard
Theological Review* 68 (1976): 83–101.

Danielou, Jean. *A History of Early Church Doctrine.* Vol. 3 of *The
Origins of Latin Christianity.* Translated by David Smith and
John Baker. Philadelphia: Westminster Press, 1977.

Evans, Robert F. *One and Holy: The Church in Latin Patristic Thought.*
London: SPCK, 1972.

Frend, W. H. C. *Saints and Sinners in the Early Church.* Wilmington,
Ind.: Michael Glazier, 1985.

Galther, Paul. *l' Eglise et la remission des peches aux primier siecles.*
Paris: Gabriel Beauchesu, 1932.

Groh, Dennis E. *Tertullian's Polemic Against Social Co-optation.*
Church History, 40. Chicago: University of Chicago Press,
1971.

Hallman, Joseph M. "The Mutability of God." *Theological Studies*
42, no. 3 (September 1981): 373–93.

Jones, P. W. "The Concept of Community in Tertullian's Writing."
Ph. D. diss., McGill University, Montreal, 1973.

Kelly, J. N. D. *Early Christian Doctrines.* London: Adam and Charles
Black, 1958.

Kelly, S. N. *Auctoritas in Tertullian: The Nature and Order of Authority
in His Thought.* Ph. D. diss., Emory University, Atlanta. Ann Arbor:
UMI, 1974.

Labriolle, Pierre Champagne de. *History and Literature of Christianity
from Tertullian to Boethius.* Translated by Herbert Wilson.
New York: Charles Scribner's Sons, 1925.

Labriolle, P. C. de *Histoire de la literature Latine Chretienne.* Vol. 1.
Paris: Societe D'Edition "Les Belle-Lettres," 1947.

Ladner, Gerhart B. *The Idea of Reform: Its Impact on Christian
Thought and Action in the Age of the Fathers.* Cambridge:
Harvard University Press, 1959.

Laistner, M. L. *Christianity and Pagan Culture in Later Roman Empire.*
Ithaca, N.Y.: Cornell University Press, 1951.

Langstadt, E. "Some Observation on Tertullian's Legalism." In *Studia Patristica*. Vol. 6. Edited by F. L. Cross. Berlin: Akademie-Verlag, 1962.

————. "Tertullian's Doctrine of Sin and Power of Absolution in 'de Pudicitia.' " In *Studia Patristica*. Vol. 2. Edited by Kurt Aland and F. L. Cross. Berlin: Akademie-Vertag, 1957.

Moignt, Joseph. "Le etude du vocabularie doctrinal de Tertullian." In *Recherches de secience Religiouse* (Paris) 52 (1964): 248–60.

Monceaux, Paul. *Histoire Literaure De l'Afrique Christiene: Depuisles Origines Jusqu'a L'ainvasion Arabe*. Tome. I. Paris: Culture et Civilization, 1963.

Osborn, E. F. "Paul and Plato in Second Century Ethics." In *Studia Patristica*. Vol. 1.5. Edited by E. A. Livingstone. Berlin: Akademie-Verlag, 1984.

Prestige, George L. *God in Patristic Thought*. London: SPCK, 1952.

Rezette, J. *La Condition de Chretien d'apres le "De Baptismo" de Tertullian*. Rome: Antonionam, 1974.

Roberts, Robert E. *The Theology of Tertullian*. London: Epworth Press, 1924.

Scullard, H. H. *Early Christian Ethics in the West from Clement to Ambrose*. London: Williams and Norgate, 1907.

Shortt, Christopher de la. *The Influence of Philosophy on the Mind of Tertullian*. London: SCM, 1933.

Starkoff, Carl F. "American Indian Religion and Religio-Cultural Identity." In *Liberation, Revolution and Freedom*. Edited by Thomas McFadden. New York: Seabury Press, 1975.

Stead, Christopher. *Substance and Illusion in the Christian Fathers*. London: Variorum Reprints, 1985.

Stead, G. C. "Divine Substance in Tertullian." *Journal of Theological Studies* 14 (April 1963): 46–66.

Stegman, C. A. B. *The Development of Tertullian's Doctrine of Spiritus Sanctus*. Ph.D. diss., Southern Methodist University, 1978. Ann Arbor: UMI, 1978.

Tibiletti, Carto. *Note Critiche al Testo de Tertulliano "de Testimonio."* Vol. 12. Naples: Giornale Italian in di Teologia.

————. *Q. S. F. Tertullian's De Testimonis: Animae: Introduction testo e commentare*. Torino: Univ. di Torino Puse Faciltad, di lettre e Filosofia, 1959.

Warfield, Benjamin B. *Studies in Tertullian and Augustine*. Westport, Conn.: Greenwood Press, 1970.

Waszink, J. H. *Quinti Florentis Tertullainus: [De Anima] With Introduction and Commentary*. Amsterdam: J. M. Meulenhoff, 1947.

Wiles, Maurce. *The Christian Fathers.* Norwich, England: SCM Press, 1977.

THEOLOGY

Barth, Karl. *Church Dogmatics*. Vol. 1.1. Edited by Geoffrey W. Bromily and T. F. Torrance. Edinburgh: T. and T. Clark, 1975.

Cone, James H. "Freedom, History, and Hope." In *Liberation Revolution and Freedom*. Edited by Thomas M. MacFadden. New York: Seabury Press, 1975.

Heyward, Isabel Carter. *Our Passion for Justice*. New York: Pilgrim Press, 1984.

————. *The Redemption of God: A Theology of Mutual Relation*. Washington, D.C.: University Press of America, 1982.

Lonergan, Bernard. *Method in Theology*. New York: Seabury Press, 1972.

McFague, Sally. *Metaphorical Theology: Models of God in Religious Language*. Philadelphia: Fortress Press, 1982.

Neibuhr, H. Richard. *Radical Monotheism and Western Culture*. New York: Harper and Row, 1970.

Neibuhr, Reinhold. *The Children of Light and the Children of Darkness*. London: Nisbet and Co., 1945.

Norris, R. A. *God and World in Early Christian Theology*. New York: Seabury Press, 1965.

Quacquarrelli, A. *La Cultara Indigena di Tertullian e i Tertullianisti de Carthagine*. Rome: Vetera Christianorum Beri, 1973.

Rambaux, Claude. *Tertullien face aux Morales da Trois primier siecles,* Paris: Societe de Education "Les Belles Lettres," 1979.

Schleiermacher, Friedrich. *The Christian Faith*. Edited by H. R. MacKintosh and J. S. Stewart. Translated by D. M. Baillie, et al. Edinburgh: T. and T. Clark, 1928.

————. *On the Discrepancy Between the Sabellian and Athanasian Method of Representing the Doctrine of the Trinity in the Godhead*. Translated by M. Stuart. Andover, Maryland: n.p., 1835.

Suchocki, Marjorie. *God, Christ, Church.* New York: Crossroad, 1989.
Tillich, Paul. *Life and the Spirit: History and the Kingdom of God.*
Vol. 3 of *Systematic Theology.* Chicago: University of
Chicago Press, 1963.
———. *Reason and Revelation* Vol. 1. of *Systematic Theology.*
Chicago: University of Chicago Press, 1951.
Tracy, David. *The Analogical Imagination.* New York: Crossroad,
1981.
———. *Blessed Rage for Order.* New York: Seabury Press, 1975.

TRINITY

Boff, Leonardo. *Trinity and Society.* Translated by Paul Burns.
Maryknoll, N.Y.: Orbis Books, 1988.
Camntwell, Lewis. *The Theology of the Trinity.* Notre Dame: Fides
Publishers, 1969.
Cousins, Ewert. "The Trinity and the World Religions." *Journal of
Ecumenical Studies* 7 (1970): 476–98.
deMargerie, Bertrand. *The Christian Trinity in History.* Translated by
Edmund J. Fortmann. Stillriver, Miss.: Saint Bede's
Publications, 1982.
Durant, Michael. *Theology and Intellibility: An Examination of the
Proposition that God is the Last End of Rational Creatures
and the Doctrine That God is Three Persons in One Substance.*
London: Routledge and Kegan Paul, 1973.
Fortmann, Edmund J. *The Triune God: A Historical Study of the
Doctrine of the Trinity.* Grand Rapids, Mich.: Baker Book House,
1972.
Hill, Edmund. *The Mystery of the Trinity.* London: Geoffrey
Chapman, 1985.
Hill, William J. *The Three Personned God.* Washington D.C.: Catholic
University Press, 1982.
Hodgson, Peter C. *God in History: Shapes of Freedom.* Nashville:
Abingdon, 1989.
MacKenzie, Charles S. *The Trinity and Culture.* New York: Peter
Lang, 1987.
Mackey, James P. *The Christian Experience of God as Trinity.* London:
SCM Press, 1983.
Moltmann, Jurgen. *The Trinity and the Kingdom.* Translated by
Margaret Kohl. San Francisco: Harper and Row, 1981.

Novatian. *The Trinity.* In *The Fathers of the Church.* Vol. 67. Translated
by Russell J. DeSimone. Washington, D.C.: Catholic
University of America Press, 1974.

Pannikar, Raimundo. *The Trinity and the Religious Experience of Man.*
Maryknoll, N.Y.: Orbis Books, 1973.

OTHER SOURCES

Adler, Mortimer J., et al. *The Great Ideas: A Synopticon of the Great
Books.* Vol. 1. Chicago: William Benton Pub., Encyclopedia
Britannica, 1986.

Aichele, George. *Limit of Story.* Philadelphia: Fortress Press, 1985.

Allen, Grant. *The Evolution of the Idea of God: An Inquiry into the
Origins of Religion.* New York: Henry Holt and Co., 1897.

Allport, Floyd H. *Theories of Perception and the Concept of Structure.*
New York: John Wiley and Sons, 1955.

Aristophanes, *The Clouds. Great Books of the Western World.* Vol. 5.
Edited by Robert M. Hutchins, et al. Chicago: Encyclopaedia
Britannica, 1952.

Aristotle. *Politics.* Tranlated by Benjamin Jewett. Vol. 9 of *Great
Books of the Western World.* Edited by Robert M. Hutchins, et al.
Chicago: William Benton Publisher, 1952.

Brightman, Edgar Shefield. *Person and Reality: Introduction to
Metaphysics.* Edited by Peter A. Bertocci. New York: Ronald
Press, 1958.

Brownell, Baker. *The Human Community.* New York: Harper and
Bros., 1950.

Buber, Martin. *Between Man and Man.* Translated by Ronald G. Smith.
Boston: Beacon Press, 1955.

Cassirer, Ernst. *The Philosophy of Symbolic Forms.* Vol. 3. New Haven,
Conn.: Yale University Press, 1957.

Copplestone, Frederick. "The Cambridge Platonist." In *Hobbes to
Hume.* Vol. 5 of *History of Philosophy.* Paramus NJ.: Newman
Press, 1961.

Copplestone, F. *Ockham to Saurez.* Vol. 3 of *History of Philosophy.*
New York: Paulist Press, 1953.

———. *Wolf and Kant.* Vol. 6 of *History of Philosophy.* New York:
Paulist Press, 1960.

Derr, Thomas Sieger. *Ecology and Human Need*. Philadelphia:
Westminster Press, 1975.

Diamond, Irene., and Gloria Feman Orenstei, eds. *Reweaving the
World: The Emergence of Ecofeminism*. San Francisco: Sierra
Club Books, 1990.

Eliade, Mircea. *The Myth of the Eternal Return*. Princeton: Princeton
University Press, 1971.

————. *The Sacred and the Profane*. San Diego: Harcourt Brace
Jovanovich, 1959.

Elliot-Binns, Leonard E. *The Beginning of Western Christendom*.
Greenwich, Conn.: Seabury Press, 1957.

Eusibius, *Ecclesiastical History*. Philadelphia: R. Davis, 1833.

Farley, Edward. *Good and Evil*. Minneapolis: Fortress Press, 1990.

Forell, Georg Wofgang. *History of Christian Ethics*. Vol. 1.
Minneapolis: Dugsbuey Publishing House, 1975.

Gertz, Clifford. *The Interpretation of Cultures*. New York: Basic
Books, 1973.

"Gemeinschaft and Geselschaft." *Encyclopaedia Britannica*. 15th ed.

Gilkey, Langdon. *Naming the Whirlwind: The Renewal of God
Language*. Indianapolis: Bobbs-Merril, 1969.

Hillman, James. *Re-visioning Psychology*. New York: Harper and
Row, 1975.

Hooks, Bell. *Feminist Theory: From Center to Margin*. Boston: South
End Press, 1984.

Izard, Michel, and Piere Smith. *Between Belief and Unbelief*.
Translated by John Leavitt. Chicago: University of Chicago:
University of Chicago Press, 1982.

Jonas, Hans. *Gnostic Religion*. Boston: Beacon Press, 1963.

Kroner, Richard. *Culture and Faith*. Chicago: University of Chicago
Press, 1951.

Libanio, J. B. *Spiritual Discernment and Politics*. Trans. Theodore
Morrow. Maryknoll, N.Y.: Orbis Books, 1982.

Lowrie, Walter. Editor's introduction to Sören Kierkegaard, *Fear and
Trembling*. Princeton: Princeton University Press, 1952.

Ochshorn, Judith. *The Female Experience and the Nature of the Divine*.
Bloomington: Indiana University Press, 1981.

Oliver, Harold H. "Relational Ontology and Hermeneutics." In *Myth,
Symbol, and Reality*. Edited by Alan M. Olson. Notre Dame
Ind.: University of Notre Dame Press, 1980.

Ricoeur, Paul. *Time and Narrative*. Vols. 1 and 3. Translated by
    Kathleen McLaughlin and David Pellauer. Chicago:
    University of Chicago Press, 1984.
Sidgwick, Henry. *Outlines of the History of Ethics*. London:
    Macmillan, 1949.
Widgery, Alban G. *Christian Ethics in History and Modern Life*. New
    York: Round Table Press, 1940.

INDEX

A

Absolute: monotheism 54; omnipotence 20; oneness of God 80; openness 9; personal attributes 42; personal rulership as 64–65; singularistic, personalistic God 13–15

Abstract: concept of personality 19; God conceived as 40; *ratio* as not merely 67

Abstractions: compared to real personifying entities 69; Divine community not 79; from Valentinian 62

Actualization: and self-realization 69; of the One throught personifications 27

African Christianity: early *xiii*; in the mind of Tertullian 51; separation from *ix*; Tertullian's 89; African cosmology: and Greek philosophy 80; as background to Tertullian *xi*

African cultures: communality of *xi*; sociologist, anthropologist and *xviii*

African Fathers: of the church 56

African Ontology *xvii*; and cosmology 29, 59

African thought: about the divine 23; the One in 25; traditional *ix*, 20

African worldview: and spirit 71; and the concept of vital force 80; Bracken's thought compared with *xvi–xviii*; common 20; community as foundational to 1, 20, 23, 89; context of *ix*; from an *xiv*; influence on the development of christianity *xix*; of the divine 29; mutual relation in 8; regard for the parent in 68; related to the 52; Tertullian's trinity and *xi*, 80

Akan (of Ghana), a study of belief and practice of the 94; divinities are called 29; doctrine of God 16–18, 31,

Consciousness: African *xiii*; and
the unspoken word 69;
cosmic 10; human *x*;
religious *xiv* 41; spirit
and *xii*

Contexts: African 8, 14, 19, 29,
42; communal 89; Divinity
in African 23; Becoming in
African 24; religious 26;
variety of 24

Conversation: about the nature
of the Divine *x*; African
contributions to   on the
trinity *xix*; between Smith and
an African priest 26; with
Kunene 29

Cosmological: emanations 62;
representation of the trinity
61; Trinity 58, 82

Cosmos (*see also* universe):
historical epochs of the 83;
man and 96; sacred
movements of the 30; the
whole 14; understanding of
the *xi*

Creation: actual experience of
70; before the   of the
world 39; context of 58;
Godhead prior to *xiv*, 61, 67;
in the beginning before 62;
of the cosmos 83; of the
world 24, 67; ordered to
community 10; the   of the
Divine 29, 91

D

Danielou, Jean *n.*, 74; on
angelmorphic christology 83;

on Tertullian's avoidance of
confusion the Son as
generated and non-
generated beings 84, 98

Danquah, Joseph B., Akan
doctrine of God 15–20, 47, 92;
and Idowu' emphasis on
monotheism 23; on
plurality of gods 22, 92

Daughter of heaven 30

Daughters of God 28–29

De Rouge 34

Degeneration: in the
understanding of God 34;
of the nature of the divine 40

Degrees of Godhood 83

DeMagerie, Betrand 72–73, 75

Dialectic: playful 75;
Tertullian's introduces 69

Dickson, Kwesi 1, African
theology 92; on the
problem of relation between
God and gods 16

Differentiated: in name 17;
through generative
impulses 36; non-
transcendentally 69

Dinka (people of Africa): Divine
unity and multiplicity 25;
92–93

Discourse; on God 22; on the
divine *x*; Theological *ix*, *xv*, 94

Dispensation: we call the
oikonomia 60, 68

Dispositio: and oikonomia 64; as
used by Tertullian 68–69;
of the divine intelligence 56

Godness: as force common to the gods 84; Divinity and 35; fact of 43

Gods: community of *xii*; divided ontologically 80, 82–84; Egyptian 33–47; existence of other 54; future in the 8; in historical context *xi, xiii*; not impassable 67; of Africa 13–30; or persons 70; personal 60; are not separated 89; temporality of the gods 6; three 64, 83, 93

Gradus: and the term persona 82; of godhood 85

Greek: and Roman 53; and the Divine oikonomia 65, 68; hypostasis 75; logos christology 61; metaphysical hierarchy *xiv*; philosophy 51, 80; the term ousia 77

Ground: adequate ground for *xi*; ontological *xvii*; genuine 5; of Mbiti's aphorism 14; nonpersonal 36; of change 80; of permanence 80; of Tertullian's conception of the inner trinitarian community 68

H

Harnack, Adolf von 78–79

Heidegger, Martin *xi–xii*, 96

Heresy: irrational deduction did not create 64; orthodoxy and 60

Hermeneutical bondage *x, xv*

Hierarchical: distribution of responsibility is not 29;

paradigm *xiii*; responsibility 22

Hierarchy of nature 22

Historical: acts of God 53; activities and appearances 78; manifestation 82; and socio-cultural conditioning 51; and temporal 85; center 35; circumstance 40; communal strictures and processes subject 6, 71; context 42; -cultural situation *xiii*; -economic 75; experiment 9; situations 43; formation of the trinity *ix*; functions 61, 63, 69; generative prolation 68, 101

History: Akan 17; ancient Egyptian 43; connection to 83, 91; divine procession in 67–70; emergence of 63; God in 53; greatly aided by conscious memory 6; initiation of 60; of creation 62; points in 24; redemptive *xiv*, 95, 98, 100–103, 105

Holy Spirit: being the utmost expression of love 71; divine in Christ and *xiv*; emphasis on the 57; father, son and the 59, 75, 79, 81; God's word and the 51; historically understood 68; in the creation of humanity 55; relation of the 72; son through the *xviii*